UNFORGETTABLE

Stephanie Lycka

Unforgettable Spaces

Stephanie Lycka

I DISCOVER HOME STAGING

encompass
EDITIONS

www.encompasseditions.com

FIRST EDITION 2013

ISBN: 978-1-927664-03-2

Cataloguing in Publication
Program (CIP) information available from Library and Archives Canada
at www.collectionscanada.gc.ca

Illustrations by David Abelson
Cover design by Robert Buckland
Interior layout by Jean Shepherd

encompass
EDITIONS

Foreword

The goal of every home seller is to sell their home. Regardless of the location, type of home or condition, if it is for sale, the owner wants to sell. Stephanie Lycka understands this completely, which is why she wrote this book and why every home stager, seller and real estate agent should read it.

Because Stephanie was new to the home staging industry, when she told me she was writing this book, I have to admit, I was a bit skeptical. What I learned over time about Stephanie though, was that she had already embraced exactly what I preach: staging is marketing. In order to sell a home in the shortest amount of time for the most amount of money, you have to effectively and authentically market the property. Staging is a huge part of that. She grasped that concept instantly because she was already an extraordinary marketer.

In this book, Stephanie Lycka's creative and often humorous approach shows you how to stage your home, or stage a home for a client, in order to achieve the best possible results. She has pulled together a panel of real-world home-staging experts to show you what it really takes to get a home sold and she is "spot on" in her direction.

Whether you are a home stager, a real estate agent or a home seller, Stephanie Lycka has created an enjoyable, accurate, "must read" for the entire real estate industry.

Karen Schaefer,
Founder, Association of Property Scene Designers,
Manitou Springs, Colorado

To

my dad, Dr. Barry Lycka, and
to my mom, Dr. Lucie-Bernier-Lycka and
to my family, who supported me along the way

Contents

1.

In Search of the Secrets

*"The body of wisdom that stagers have accumu-
lated over recent decades is open to anyone."*

*L*et me guess. You've picked up this book because you're a home stager yourself, or you're a realtor who wants to sell a listing. Or maybe you've heard friends talking about staging and you're thinking of buying or selling a house. Wait a minute, there's another possibility: you've been watching one of those reality TV shows based (sometimes loosely) on actual staging. Whatever the case, if you're of a certain age, it's likely occurred to you that nobody you knew was talking about staging even fifteen years ago. And even if you're not thoroughly familiar with this recently-developed profession, you probably find something intriguing about its role at the interface between business transactions—the buying and selling of houses—and the softer arts of interior décor and human psychology.

In that case, you and I have something in common. I've been drawn to the arts all my life—I love the dance in all its forms, for example—and I've always had a confident sense of what makes the interiors of our houses work. But I'm grounded in a family of practical people—my father is a world-renowned cosmetic dermatologist and my mother is a respected family practitioner—and I too have aspired to develop skills that are fundamentally practical. When I discovered staging, I knew I'd found my field.

$\mathcal{I}$'m not writing this book at the culmination of a lifetime of experience—or ten years' experience, or even five. I'm a new stager, recently trained and just cutting my teeth. But as I investigated the profession—and I don't mean simply learned a few rules—I decided to describe what I've learned so far so others can accompany me on my course of discovery. For me, learning from other people and sharing knowledge with them—that's the core principle.

...house selling is increasingly competitive and truly professional home stagers do bring something special to the challenge.

I can hear you wondering, "Why is she telling me this? This author is a young home stager, not my best friend. Her business is advising people. Why would she devote a book to giving away her trade secrets to anyone who has the hour or so it takes to read this book?"

The short answer is that there are no trade secrets. The body of wisdom that stagers have accumulated over recent decades is open to anyone who's willing to explore the subject. In a rather casual and informal way, real estate agents— even ones who barely understand the subject of staging— have been passing these "secrets" on to clients for years. Their common sense has told them that it's easier to sell a house that looks good *to the person buying it.* They don't want to offend their selling clients, of course, but they'll feel an obligation to say things like, "Er, I see you let the kitties go the bathroom on the laundry room floor. Might be a good idea if they didn't...at least until the house is sold."

So it doesn't take a genius to figure this out and much of good staging consists of sense that's just as common as that. But as I hope you'll come to appreciate—if you don't already—house selling is increasingly competitive and truly professionals home stagers *do* bring something special to the challenge. That something special is what often makes the difference between tens of thousands of dollars and the loss of tens of thousands of dollars. That something special is one of the things I hope you'll discover, as I did.

Staging takes more than a certain flair—or sometimes genius—for staging design. It takes hard work, as I was to discover. And this brings me to the TV shows. In fact every stager has a love–hate relationship with the popular shows that feature the staging of homes. *The Stagers, Sell This House* and *Designed to Sell* are three popular ones in the U.S. Let's face it: they're entertaining, they open people's minds to the many possibilities for flooring, for furniture and fixtures and lighting and painting and bathroom and kitchen renovations. They give inspiration to people who like DIY projects. They see that they too can do it—quickly and easily.

There's the rub. It looks easy on TV—*way* too easy—but in fact every aspect of the sale and purchase of a home is time-consuming and challenging and staging is no exception.

Like dance, which looks easy too, it's not: it requires talent, dedication, and a passion for exacting detail.

When I watch TV staging shows, I'm always a little shocked (and amused) at how little money these radical transformations cost. The other side of this coin is that potential clients are shocked in turn at the estimate for an actual staging—not a consultation—of their home for sale. Reality and Reality TV are not the same thing? How could that be?

You must know what I'm talking about. The *Sell This House* team, for example (on the A&E Network) go through an impossible place whose owners simply don't have a clue. Tanya Memme with somewhat strenuous humour checks out the horrible paint jobs and the filthy stove and the hapless sellers watch a bunch of pretend "buyers" on "hidden" cameras gasp and gag as they tour the place before Tanya and consultant Roger Hazard and their team transform it into what everyone likens to a "luxury hotel." Total cost? A paltry eleven hundred and twenty-nine dollars.

I'm very much indebted to Beth Lester of Home Staging Designs of California for tackling this misperception. Beth has carefully broken down the costs entailed in real-world staging. She explains that home staging businesses are typically run by entrepreneurs who have significant overhead, just like any other business, large or small. Even if you don't count labour, you have to include:

♦ Inventory purchase: accessories, furniture, plants, artwork, outdoor furnishings, etc.

♦ Storage of inventory: a significant expense.

♦ Marketing costs: website, advertising materials, local ads.

♦ Insurance for the storage facility, liability, damage during transportation of goods, etc.

♦ Automotive expenses.

♦ Employee salaries and taxes.

♦ Professional fees for real estate, staging and design organizations.

♦ Continuing education costs: travel, classes and time.

♦ Usual business fees: telephone, utilities, computer and copier equipment, supplies, legal counsel, tax and accounting counsel.

♦ Rental furniture. If your stager must bring in rental furniture, the cost of that furniture must cover another business' expenses, including warehouse, storefront, employees and transportation. Furniture is typically the single largest expense in staging vacant homes.

Now all this is before the stager begins to use any of her or his own time—or someone else's. Yes, some parts of staging are fun, but a good deal of it is tiring and mundane. Let's look at Beth's breakdown on these tasks.

The Occupied Home

- ◆ Calls from client and/or the realtor to set up an appointment.
- ◆ Research of property and other properties in the area.
- ◆ Travel time.
- ◆ Actual consultation time with the client.
- ◆ Writing up checklists.
- ◆ Multiple emails and phone calls with follow-up questions and answers.
- ◆ Sometimes photographs—taking and editing them, sending them to the realtor and the client.
- ◆ Hands-on work inside the home.

The charge for all of these hours is typically between two and four hundred dollars—an awfully low hourly fee, as it works out.

The Vacant Home

Now this, as Beth says, is where the serious hours and hard work come in. She provides a blow-by-blow of the stager's toil.

- Schedule appointment.

- Travel to and from the property to preview home with the owner or agent. Consultation for recommendations are often included.

- Take pictures, make notes and measure major rooms.

- Design rough plan sufficient to make proposal. Send it to the client and call to be sure it was received.

- After acceptance, create the full design plan, make color selections and decide furniture placement.

- Choose furniture online and order available items for delivery date.

- Sign and return the contract.

- To prepare for delivery, sort through current inventory in storage facility to choose artwork, accessories, lighting, rugs, plants, candles, bedding, bath linens, etc.

- Shop to fill in any gaps. (Of course, many hours were spent earlier to purchase and maintain all those items).

- Now wrap everything up and prepare to deliver.

- Make as many trips as necessary and wait to meet furniture delivery truck. (Don't forget to tip the guy well!)

- Lug every box and item into the property, sometimes far from the parking lot, down hallways, or up and down stairs.

- Unwrap and place each item. Sometimes it takes several tries to find the perfect place. Hang all artwork (How long does that take *you*?)

- ♦ Steam and press linens as necessary.
- ♦ Once the home has been transformed, clean up and load all the supplies and boxes back into the car, to be unloaded and re-sorted back at the storage facility.
- ♦ Take "after" photographs, which are then selected, edited, sent to realtor and owner.
- ♦ Create a slideshow and flyers and post to real estate websites.
- ♦ Write marketing pieces and blogs to promote the newly staged home to all recipients on the database.
- ♦ When the home is sold and ready to go to its new owner, the stager returns to the property to repack all items, wait for the furniture truck, load up and return to the storage facility where each item must be restocked, ready to repeat the process for the next staging.
- ♦ Finish up all job-related book work: filing and recording of receipts, invoicing payments, banking, etc.

A good, caring home stager will typically do everything possible to serve the client—going above and beyond the call of duty.

Tired yet?

So how, Beth Lester asks, can they transform a home, including construction changes, for eleven hundred and twenty-nine dollars on A&E or HGTV?

The answer is: commercials.

"Every designer, carpenter, landscape designer, sewing

professional, lighting technician, workman and host on these programs is paid for by the commercials we watch. There are assistants performing every job from selecting furniture, working with rental companies to use their furniture (apparently without the minimum that real life stagers have to work with), hunting down bargains at thrift stores, shopping for paint. You name it, someone is doing it, but they don't show that on TV and it is not included in the cost given. So the real value of what they do is *thousands* of dollars—and the final product brings many more thousands in return on their investment."[1]

Most of these staging shows aren't going to tell you that buying a new house can take maybe months, with plenty of mortgage and legal work along the way. They're not going to tell you that adding a few pieces of furniture is not enough and that staging requires specific accessories that target specific buyers. They aren't going to tell you that it can take weeks to even *find* a contractor you can afford, and even when you find someone they may do a lousy job or need to be constantly hassled to finish the job. The shows' message often seems to be "You're an idiot but even an idiot can do this in a snap."

A good, caring home stager will typically do everything possible to serve the client—going above and beyond the call of duty.

---

[1] You can visit Beth Lester's website at http://homestagingdesignsca.com

An honourable exception is the Canadian *Holmes on Homes*, a renovation show. Mike Holmes' ultimate message seems to be that you can't—or shouldn't—do everything yourself. Real builders and real decorators and real stagers may invest years in continually upgrading their professional training, skills and education. Take advantage of it: that's what I came to understand.

Meanwhile, as I studied and listened, I realized that there was seldom total agreement about what constitutes the best staging, or even what staging means. This is still in many respects an unstructured profession. It is in many instances—by no means all—an amateur profession. Of course that has its downsides—you as a seller should know who you're dealing with—but I found the ferment of opinion and change exciting. As I got further and further into it, I began to learn about and wonder about not just the techniques of staging, but its theoretical side. What were we actually doing? Stripping a home of any evidence of the seller's personal life—what's usually called "depersonalizing?" Or letting the seller's personality and lifestyle show through in order to give the home a unique character that a buyer might identify with—what you might call "personalizing?" I noticed quite a lot of disagreement about this and I began to get a bit, well, a bit obsessed. Maybe it was watching too many staging shows, but I actually began to dream about staging.

I know, I know—that seems a bit much. But when you

stop and think about it, are dreams any stranger than reality television?

Maybe you can decide.

2.

A Star Stager

"Hmm," he wondered. "Would I stop for such a place?"

I was already a totally experienced home stager. But better than that, I didn't have to drive to people's neighbourhoods and meet them; I could just sort of float over and go down and pass into their rooms. Even better, I discovered I was able to hear the sellers' thoughts.

On this occasion, I'd just floated over to a leafy side street in the Garneau area, an older part of south-central Edmonton. I wasn't there by pure chance, it seems. Apparently I'd visited the same home "on the ground" earlier in the day. Was that in another dream or was it just in the "dream past" of this dream? Honestly, I don't know much about dreams; I'm simply reporting this one to you. Anyway, I was just hovering below the foyer ceiling, looking down at a man of about thirty-five, standing below me. I somehow knew this was James Hargreaves, the manager and part-owner of a modest but pretty successful automotive parts business in Edmonton. He was standing there looking at a cluster of sneakers near the front door.

"They're okay," he was thinking. "Everybody has feet."

"Still," I thought, "There are people who might think a pile of old sneakers was a teeny bit gross."

"Still," James thought. "They might seem sort of gross to

somebody who didn't know the family. Maybe I should put them away."

"This is wonderful," I thought. "I don't have to explain anything or convince anyone and maybe offend them. Hey, I like this staging stuff."

James and his wife Robyn had two kids, three and five, and a third on the way. They also had a pleasant older house—a sort of higher-end starter home they'd occupied for four years. They'd recently seen a house in a new development, Hamborough Place, that fit all the needs of their growing family. They were now about to put their present home up for sale.

James started to pick up the sneakers but then he looked up and out the front door window.

"I think he's starting to think," I thought.

"What part of the house do prospective buyers really see first?" James wondered.

"The outside," I thought.

"The outside, of course," James thought. And now that he'd thought of it, he realized many home buyers drive around an area and have a good look at houses for sale before they even contact a realtor. After all, that was what James and Robyn did when they originally bought the place. It doesn't matter how much effort and time an owner spends decorating the interior, if a prospective buyer doesn't like what they see when they drive by, they'll never ask to see inside that home.

"That would be unfair," James was thinking. "That would be like some heartless municipal tax inspector driving by and assessing our house at too high a value. Only this would be the opposite—a drive-by under-assessment."

"First impressions count with houses," I hinted. "Just like they do with people. The clothes make the man and the outside makes the home."

"You know what?" James thought. "It's the outside that tempts a prospective buyer to come inside."

And he went outside and looked at his house. I was right above him.

"Pretty nice house," he thought.

"With a few little problems," I thought.

He stood back.

"Alright," he was thinking. "The gutters are full of leaves and there's that one loose shingle. But could anyone driving by possibly think that the place wasn't well maintained based on little things like that?"

"Yes," I thought.

He looked down the street where two neighbours had their houses for sale. They were all built about the same time. He squinted but he couldn't actually make out any leaves in the gutters—or broken shingles.

"Better see to that," he thought. "And maybe while I'm at it I'll go all the way out to the curb and look back. They do call it curb appeal, don't they?"

"Yes, they do," I thought.

James stood at the curb.

"Things look pretty good from there," he congratulated himself. "Of course the lawn's a thing of beauty because I always knew a scruffy lawn was a turn-off for anyone. Okay, maybe there's a little teeny flaw—the swing set off in the right corner. The kids have worn the lawn a bit bare there. But heck, lots of people have kids and kids need a place to play. Who'd be bothered by a little bare ground under a good-quality swing set?"

"See a lot of bare patches on other lawns?" I wondered. "See a lot of little kids?"

James looked up the street. Three houses had sold there that spring. All of them were purchased by families with older children. The high school was only two blocks away and the community college was about a mile west. He looked back at the swing set and the little muddy puddle under it.

"Okay. It probably wouldn't be that hard to dismantle it, just for a few weeks."

"Perfect."

While he was thinking that, he was also thanking his foresight—his lucky stars, more like—that he had had the brickwork pointed two years ago. These houses were built in the nineteen thirties and some were starting to show signs of time passing.

"Still, it looks great overall," he reassured himself.

"The trim?"

"Hmm. Okay, too bad about the trim, though it's fine, really. All it needs is a coat of paint. Maybe the new owner will want to do it."

"Oh sure," I thought. "Like new owners these days want to start doing maintenance the moment they move in."

James kept a note pad in his pocket for business purposes and now he took it out and wrote "trim?" Below that, he wrote, "Replace broken electrical outlet." Below that he wrote "Replace rusty mailbox" and then "Discard Christmas wreath."

Now, in this dream, I knew James's wife Robyn had spent quite a lot of effort on the front garden, so that was a bonus, of course.

I thought. "Like new owners these days want to start doing maintenance the moment they move in."

"What about those cedars she wanted?" I mused.

"Wonder if there might be any cedars left at the nursery?" I heard James wondering. "That would be the sort of artistic touch that would really polish things off."

He squinted again and imagined the place with those changes.

"Hmm," he wondered. "Would I stop for such a place?" He hesitated. "Yes, I would," he thought.

"Oh yeah?" I thought. "Why?"

He was nodding to himself with approval. "One of the

terrific things our place has going for it is that the lot is wid-
er than most of the neighbours and you can see right through
at the side to the landscaped back garden and the miniature
orchard."

"Oh yeah?"

"Well, normally you can, except that broken tool shed's still
waiting for GotJunk to haul it away. "Call GotJunk" he wrote.

On the whole, he still seemed pleased, but for the first
time he was a teeny bit insecure, which was good. There
were quite a few houses for sale at the moment in the area.
How would his and Robyn's stand up?

Now James surprised me by walking out to his car, getting
in and driving off. I love dreams where I'm riding in cars but
this was especially cool: I was floating above the car.

We drove around the neighbourhood

"This is just what buyers do, isn't it?" he was thinking.
He drove very slowly by the other houses with for-sale signs
on the lawn. Three of them were looking pretty good. One
seemed a bit shabby. Why? He stopped and studied the exterior. Several shingles were loose—nothing more.

"What's that tell you?" I wondered.

He drove back to his own house and stopped.

"See anything?" I wondered.

"Funny," James thought. "I'd forgotten about that piece of
an old television antennae. It's been sticking up beside the
chimney for dog's years. It's like I didn't notice that stuff with

Abelson

my own house. "Nix the TV ant" he wrote.

You know how dreams are. One minute I was watching James study his old antenna, the next he and his wife Robyn were in the kitchen talking about curb appeal—and I was there, hovering. James was listing his projects. Robyn was punching buttons on the microwave.

"James," Robyn was saying. "This is impressive. I'm amazed you've come around about this."

"I dunno," James agreed. "Something just inspired me."

"Great, but don't put away your pencil. Write down that we have to wash all the windows as soon as the sign goes up. I mean really wash them—inside and out—so they sparkle. Then we'll need to walk around and inspect every window to make sure there's nothing, you know, embarrassing showing. Stuff that's been on the sills for a year, broken lampshades peeking out. That sort of thing."

"Really?"

"And we've got to do something about that front door."

"No kidding? It always worked when I opened it."

"Don't be amusing, darling. This is the door people enter the house through. It sums up the whole home. What sort of message is it sending now?"

"A happy home?"

She smiled affectionately but sadly.

"Well, yes. Happy and grubby. I'm afraid it's got to gleam."

"Gleam?"

"The door handle and the knocker. They don't gleam."

"Okay okay."

He wrote "Door must gleam."

"And we need to rent a power washer and really do a number on that driveway and front walk. And all the kids' toys and bikes and everything will have to be put away."

"But how are the little dears supposed to live?" James wondered.

"Well, I was thinking about that. How about we designate a place in the basement and store everything there really neatly and see that every single thing is put away every day?"

"Phew," he said. "Whose house do these buyers think it is, anyway?"

Robyn smiled and punched the on button and the microwave hummed.

"We want them to think it's theirs," she said.

I hovered over them, smiling, proud to have influenced Robyn during my earlier visit, which hadn't happened in the dream, you understand, but for sure I was dreaming that it had happened.

"I know this staging seems like a hassle," Robyn was saying. "But what if we don't sell the house right away? Imagine it drags on and on until it's stale on the market? How will we be able to put the deposit on Hamborough Place?"

James looked somber. He wanted that house in Hamborough Place.

"Anyway," Robyn added. "That's why I've asked Stephanie over. She should be here any moment."

"Who's Stephanie?" James asked.

I experienced quite a shock, believe me. Here I was hovering over these people and one of them suddenly reminds me I'm supposed to be at the front door of their house.

"Stephanie Lycka? You haven't heard of her?" Robyn wondered. "She's a famous home stager. We're very lucky to get her, James. She said she'd stop by about now and give us a quick consultation."

I know this seems like cheating because it was my dream, but you know what its like with dreams. They don't feel like you're making them up.

"Robyn," James was saying. "We want to sell our house, dear, not put on a play. Now that we've got an agent, let's just sign the contract, put up the sign and sell it."

"Actually, it was the agent, Craig, who suggested I speak to Stephanie."

"Really?"

At that moment the front doorbell chimed and I knew it must be me. I immediately swooshed out of the house, circled above the front lawn and settled outside the front door.

"You know what?" I could hear Robyn saying as she approached the door. "I'm not so sure that we're not putting on a play."

As I walked through the front entranceway, I had a sort

of dream déjà-vu, which made sense because, as I say, I'd apparently visited earlier that dream-day. I looked around and right away, I really liked James' and Robyn's taste in interiors.

"I love your taste," I said. Maybe that wasn't so surprising, since it was me who was dreaming this home. "But do you think we should go outside and look at the house from there?"

"Actually," James explained, "I've done that myself and Robyn here has added a whole list of things. I think the outside is going to be fine."

"Of course," I assured him. But I didn't want him getting a swollen head. "I love that you've already given it some thought. Let's just take a minute though and see if I have anything I can add. A second set of eyes cant hurt, right?"

We stood on the front driveway. James noticed me looking at the oil stains and took out his list and read it aloud.

"That's great," I said. "And the power washer is a terrific idea. But you know what you may find? After you've cleaned the drive and the walk and the siding and everything, you're going to start to notice things you hadn't noticed before."

"I know, I know," James said. The trim. But I noticed it already."

"And?"

"You don't think the buyer would like to paint it, do you?" He looked hopeful. "I mean, paint it his or her own colour?"

I gave him a kindly smile.

"You know, James, something I've learned in my many

many years as a home stager is that buyers today don't want to do much at all."

"You mean they want to walk into a perfect place?"

"I'm afraid so. But you're making an important point. Preparing a house for sale has got to be cost effective. So of course you want to balance the cost of painting all the trim against your objective."

"You mean we want to make the house look as good as possible, right?"

"No no. That's not your objective. You could go on working and spending forever if it was. That's interior decorating, which is something totally different. Your real objective is to sell your house as quickly as possible at the highest reasonable price."

Preparing a house for sale has got to be cost effective.

"Hmm." James was looking at me with a touch of awe, but apparently I was used to this, as a famous stager. "That's true, isn't it?" he wondered.

"So let's just walk around," I suggested. "Let's just consider what could be done and then balance it against the advantages."

And so we did. I showed them how to look at the house not as his and Robyn's house but through the eyes of a potential buyer. I poked at the back of the house where a patch of siding had rotted and cracked. I found mold and mildew around two window wells. I scratched at the mortar between

colours. I wish more people would install them when they put their house on the market. I like the birdbath too. These features—little ponds and that sort of thing—are extremely attractive to almost all buyers. You just have to know where to stop."

"Like deep-sixing the gnomes," Robyn said.

"Right. and the flamingoes and so on. They cross a line—I call it the "art line"—and you risk turning off your potential buyers. Art is just so personal."

I glanced at my watch which, being a dream watch, had a dollar sign but no hands.

"Oh dear. I'm supposed to be somewhere else. We're moving a set of restrained furnishings into a home in Bridesdale. The owners' taste is pretty much over the top. I mean beyond acceptable. You understand, I'm sure."

"I totally understand," Robyn said. "At some point, we women have to take control."

We walked to the car.

"I'll come back if you like," I said. "I guess I just want to leave you with this. It's not that there's anything wrong with our houses the way we live in them. But when we're showing them to buyers, we have to recognize that buyers interpret stuff. A smell or a broken window take on a sort of symbolic meaning. They say "neglect" to the buyer. That's why we go beyond everyday house keeping when we're staging. Houses are expensive things. Discounting them is expensive too."

"Stephanie." Robyn took my hand. "I just want to say that you're everything we could have hoped for in a stager. Thank you. Thank you." There were tears in her eyes.

James also seemed moved. "I wonder if the plant nursery is still open," he wondered aloud.

"It has been wonderful," I said. "Good-bye, both of you."

"Good-bye, Stephanie!"

James and Robyn waved in unison. I rose gently into the air and then swept up and over the rooftops. Below, they were still waving.

3.

The Stager from Hell

Patty's eyes narrowed.
"Who would buy such a house?"

I admit it. I'd probably been thinking about staging too hard. You know when you've gone over the top because thing's start to turn dark. A few weeks later I found myself one night in a sort of Edmonton, which also looked like a sort of Vancouver and Toronto. These people were trying to sell their house but I don't know why I was there because they'd already engaged a home stager.

From somewhere I could hear desperation in a man's voice and there was another voice in the background, a sort of barking voice. I was floating down in a totally affluent neighbourhood with trees a hundred feet high on the front lawns and I saw a name on the mailbox, one of those roadside mailboxes like you normally see in the country. "Nick & Johanna Knakk" it said on the side of the box. I remember the spelling.

The front door swung open and I swooped in. Nick and Johanna were standing in the foyer. He was a slight, carefully dressed man in his mid-forties with receding hair. She was tall, intellectual-looking blonde. Their body language was anxious. Then I realized someone else was with them. I recognized her immediately: Patty, the Stager from Hell.

"Thank you so much, Patty," Nick was saying.

"It's my style," the Stager from Hell was saying. She was a

sturdy woman of about fifty, dressed in a gray, no-nonsense skirt and jacket. I noticed her chin jutted slightly. "My terrific style," she added. "It's what I am. I'm just truthful about the way people live."

"We deserve it, everything you say," Johanna was saying.

I touched down and looked around. Nick and Johanna's house was unusual, even by the standards of a dream, which maybe I didn't know I was having at the time. But somehow I did know they'd inherited a lot of money from Johanna's mother and travelled all around the world collecting stuff. Now they wanted to sell because they'd bought a castle in Ireland with more room.

The high walls were lined with these humongous glass cabinets filled with Ming porcelain and Victorian dolls and stuffed tropical birds and jewelry. The furniture was terribly old and elaborately carved. There were so many old masters paintings, they were hung four deep on wires attached to the ceilings. Also hanging were these amazing baskets of tropical flowers and the scent was enough to make your head spin, it was so rich and exotic.

"This home is presentable from the curb," Patty was saying. "It's inviting to the buyer even though the clock in the clock tower is showing ten minutes fast. But curb appeal is no good if the home doesn't follow through and the first impression of the home after the curb appeal is the front entry. That impression should be of a clean, inviting space that smells fresh and welcoming." She wrinkled her nose with distaste. "Sellers must exercise restraint with air fresheners. Sweet, cloying smells will not encourage the buyer to stay and look around. There are many people now with asthma and allergies, so care should be taken to use fresheners that will not aggravate these conditions."

She tilted her head and squinted at the wall to the

"Make the entryway look large and by all means without clutter."

left of the front entrance, where a dozen mounted heads of moose, elk and bucks, antelope and one tiger were arrayed above the fireplace. A little silk jacket, probably Johanna's, dangled casually from a prong of a low-hung antelope horn.

"If there's a coat rack or shelf in the front entrance, it may detract from the appeal of the entryway," Patty reminded them. "The first impression a seller wants to create is a space that is large, clean, and flowing into the rest of the house."

"I've always thought it was *pretty* large," Nick volunteered.

"Avoid distractions at the moment of entry," said Patty. "Tables or shelves in the entryway should have only one or two items on them—an arrangement of flowers or a statuette at most."

"Could we keep the Giacomettis?" Johanna wondered.

"One at most. And there should be no pictures on the wall," she added, waving a bejeweled hand at the score or so that were hung there. "Make the entryway look large and by all means without clutter."

page 48

"No clutter," Nick said. He also was scribbling on a pad.

"Clutter." Patty shook her head. "Everybody has it. Some have it worse than others. Dreadful. Sad. The problem with clutter is that it totally obscures the charm of a home."

"I know," Nick said. He was looking down, shuffling his feet. "Before you came along, we'd thought the *clutter* was charming."

"How wrong is *that*?" Patty snorted. "Really. A prospective buyer may walk into a home based on the curb appeal, but clutter tells that buyer that the home has not been well cared for. Clutter drives buyers *from* a home. Clutter and uncleanliness causes them to turn around and walk right back out."

"We have three cleaning ladies," Johanna said, her voice soft.

Patty let out a bark of a laugh and swept her arm to encompass the room. "They didn't clean out *this* stuff, did they?" She marched across the foyer and flung open a big oak closet door. The closet was dark but small avalanche of antique tennis rackets and African sculpture slid from somewhere and lay on the floor. Patty gazed at them with contempt.

"The temptation of a seller with a cluttered home," she said, "is to shove the clutter into a closet. A real buyer will *always* open all doors and check out storage spaces. The seller has but one task." She raised her voice. *"To get rid of the clutter so that the entire property can be shown to the best advantage!"*

There was a set of built-in drawers under the grand staircase. Patty opened each one and emptied its contents onto the floor.

"A closet or drawer that is stuffed with unnecessary rubbish gives the buyer the impression that there is not enough storage space in the house," she muttered, apparently absorbed in her work. "Storage! Storage is what buyers are looking for! Surely that's obvious."

"You're right, Patty," Nick mumbled.

She swept past him. "Where's the kitchen?" she demanded.

They set off down a long, oak-paneled hallway lined with paintings.

"Buyers don't care about your personal belongings," Patty said. "The don't care about your collections. It's all clutter."

"Buyers don't care about your personal belongings," Patty said. "The don't care about your collections. It's all clutter. They want to see your *house*. Without clutter, a space looks larger and more inviting." She opened another door, rolled her eyes, slammed it shut. "If a buyer opens a closet full of clutter, the buyer immediately thinks there's not enough storage space in the house. The buyer may not recognize the clutter for what it is: clutter. They may not realize that in fact there's plenty of storage—*plenty*."

We entered a vast space with what seemed to be a forest canopy overhead. I sensed that exotic birds were flitting unseen through the branches. Around the walls, all the appliances were gleaming stainless steel but bigger than normal. A wood fire roared in a towering stone fireplace.

"We're sorry about all this," Nick said.

Patty stood with her hands on her hips.

"The most important room in the house to a woman buyer is the kitchen. If there is not enough space in the kitchen, there will be no need to look at the rest of the house. Some buyers will begin in the kitchen and *never* go any farther."

"I wouldn't go farther," Nick confessed.

"When looking at the kitchen in a home, what is it that the buyer wants to see?" Patty asked. "What is it that the buyer is buying? Not your awful eighteenth-century dishes or your ridiculous solid-silver flatware, not your copper pots and pans. The buyer is buying the space for her *own personal belongings*. Any kitchen must maximize the space available and show it to its best advantage. It's the *space* I'm talking about!"

For the first time I noticed one soaring wall was filled entirely with glass-fronted cabinets and drawers that rose maybe twenty feet and appeared to be crafted from cherry wood. Patty scrambled up the ladders provided and opened each door in turn.

"Cabinets must be clean and clear of clutter and debris," she panted. "Dishes should be stacked artfully so that they give a view of the space available. When a buyer looks in your drawers, she wants to see organization, not a hundred different gadgets stuffed in."

She hurled down a shower of sieves, can openers, pencils, notebooks, egg slicers.

"Is there a pantry?" she called.

Johanna blushed. "Well, there is one over this way, I suppose."

Patty came down the ladder and marched straight through a sort of arch, with Johanna and Nick following. I trailed behind, feeling pretty bad for the offending couple, but nobody really seemed to care how I felt, or even knew I was there.

The pantry was proportionally huge, like a small warehouse, and there were a dozen extremely small people scurrying about, restocking shelves and checking bins. Patty rolled her eyes.

"Puu-leeze! The buyer needs to see *all* the shelves and storage bins completely unobstructed!" She seized a broom and with two or three broad strokes, swept the little people up and sent them squealing into the dark recesses of the room. "A cluttered pantry, with half-used boxes of crackers and cereal, cans stacked carelessly on shelves, even cleaning tools thrown in—that's not going to allow a buyer to visualize their own immaculate items shelved and neatly arranged. Is it? *Is it?*"

She pushed past us without waiting for an answer and returned to the main kitchen, where three chefs in tall white hats cowered behind potted plants. For the first time I noticed the hundreds of copper pots and pans—the kind you see in French interior decor magazines—were hung in festoons from above. Patty waggled a finger at them.

"The storage area for pots and pans should be arranged so that the buyer can see the flow of work within the kitchen, right? And see herself working in the space, right?" She cast a cold eye along the almost endless array of glowing copper. "If pots and pans are left visible, the storage should be neat and clean and complement the decor of the kitchen, not detract from it. Is that what I'm seeing?"

"I knew we had it wrong!" poor Nick cried in what looked like real anguish. "You can't see the flow of work at all!"

Patty swung around and cast a still-baleful eye on the counter tops, which stretched into the distance like airport runways made of black granite. She turned back to Johanna and Nick with a fierce glare.

"Is it so difficult to understand that buyers are looking for kitchens that maximize counter space?" she asked. "Countertops must be clear of all clutter to allow a buyer to envision their own splendid and very personal items in the kitchen and judge whether the space is adequate to accommodate those items."

She clambered abruptly onto the counter and mounted a small electric vehicle that was waiting there. She accelerated with a lurch and steered precariously the length of that countertop, kicking La Gondola pasta makers and La Pavoni espresso machines to the floor as she went.

"It looks much better now!" Johanna thrilled.

Patty drove back and descended. Her face glowed with a kind of satisfaction.

"The second most important room in the house is the bathroom," she said. "Do you have one?"

"Oh yes. We have several—er, *many*," Nick said.

"Take me to the master bathroom!"

I personally thought the bathroom's most striking feature was the two-storey waterfall at the distant end. But Patty had more pressing staging issues in mind.

"A buyer wants to see that the bathrooms are *functional*. I don't think that's too much to ask, is it? Buyers want to know bathrooms will meet their needs: their showering, their shaving, their brushing of teeth, their everything else. If the potential buyers have children, they will want to be sure there is enough space in the bathrooms to store medicines, toiletries and cosmetics as well as linens and towels."

"Oh yes yes!" Johanna seemed genuinely relieved. "We've got all those!"

Patty's eyes narrowed. "But a buyer does *not* want to see all the personal items of the *owners*. Yes, there should be a space for shampoos, conditioners, and shaving cream or foam. But the seller's medicines, toiletries and cosmetics must be carefully and neatly stored so the genuine buyer can see how their own extremely tasteful things could be put away and not clutter their pristine future counters and shelves. The seller's personal items absolutely cannot litter windowsills or shower shelves. Who would buy such a house? Buyers must see optimal arrangements—with themselves resplendent in that arrangement!"

"I'm writing all this down!" Nick cried.

Patty stepped up onto the toilet seat and addressed the room.

"Bathrooms are vital to the decision of a buyer. Bathrooms show the care and cleanliness that a potential buyer must see in a home

"The acid test for the bathroom is the ease of moving around and getting the morning dressing tasks done."

they are considering purchasing. The bathroom should have empty, empty and immaculate countertops and appliances. The tub and toilet must sparkle and the floors must be shiny and clear of obstacles."

She stepped down.

"The acid test for the bathroom is the ease of moving around and getting the morning dressing tasks done." Patty strode off in the direction of the waterfall. "If a bathroom fails in that way, it's completely useless. A bath that is too small will not allow two people to interact in the lavatory space and get teeth brushed, hair arranged, and shaving accomplished."

"Er, I think our bathroom's big enough for that," Nick interjected meekly.

But Patty was absolute.

"If not, I'm afraid all this must be torn out entirely and rebuilt with the buyer in mind!"

Nick scribbled on his pad.

We stood at the entrance to the master bedroom. An immense stained-glass rose window filled the far wall and an ancient candelabra was suspended from the domed ceiling. To the right, thousands of leather-bound volumes filled high bookcases. I totally understood that they were rare—very rare. To the left, arching windows looked out on a mountain landscape I hadn't noticed on arrival. But that's the way it is with dreams, right? You sometimes don't know how you got to the place where they start and you never ask yourself the question.

"Depersonalize, depersonalize, depersonalize!" Patty chanted. She had grown increasingly excited after leaving the bathroom. "I can't say it too often!" And indeed she couldn't. "Bedrooms are dreadfully personal. Depersonalize! The task of the seller is to depersonalize the bedroom so that the buyer can see it through their own eyes and imagine their own wonderful furniture and items in the room. And how do we depersonalize a room? You know, don't you? Yes! By getting rid of the *clutter* and eliminating as many personal items on display as possible. And *knickknacks*!"

"Yes?" said Nick, looking up from his pad.

"Knickknacks must be carefully packed away so that they do not clutter the area. Books must be beautifully arranged or packed away. Items such as teddy bears, posters, and trophies should be removed and packed away. Away! Away!"

While she spoke, I myself was standing agog at the entrance to the walk-in closet that stretched a hundred yards in length and was lined entirely with pungent cedar. Patty pushed past me.

"Closets must have a minimum of neatly arranged clothes and shoes in them. Closets crammed with clothes, shoes and extraneous items will look smaller than they really are. Clean this closet out immediately and neatly arrange a few pieces so the buyer will be able to see the space instead of the clutter. Space—that's what buyers want. Then they can visualize their own belongings *in the space*."

"Space," Nick wrote.

"And light!" Patty looked exasperated. "*Light* is what they want! Windows! Windows!" She seemed transported by a vision. She pointed at the towering bookcases. "Out with these!" she cried. "Make way for windows that will let in the light!"

"But there are two daVinci manuscripts there and a Gutenberg Bible!" Nick protested.

"Out!" Patty shouted. "Out!"

But even *she* fell silent when a distinct roaring sound echoed from a nearby part of the house.

"It's okay," Johanna said. "It's just Paw, our old leopard."

Patty's eyes grew round, then narrow.

"You...you have *pets*?"

"Oh yes," Johanna giggled. "But we don't really count Paw, he's so old. He's just lonely after we had to let Maw go. She ate too many things she shouldn't have."

Patty turned slowly. "Pets in your *home*?"

"Hundreds," Nick said proudly. "But all very well looked after."

"Where are they?" Patty asked, her own voice something of a growl.

"Right through here." Nick was already striding off, apparently oblivious.

He was right. They did seem well looked after. The ostriches in the brilliant savannah environment winked at us with placid indifference. The Brazilian macaws in the climate-controlled tropical section of the aviary fluttered from tree to tree like flying paint brushes, their screeches echoing from the glass-covered dome. The monkeys in the simian village gamboled happily while contentedly engaging in monkey business, some of it not very pretty to watch.

"We hope to add a pygmy elephant in March," Nick explained. "If, that is, we don't sell."

Patty slumped into a chair and dabbed at her forehead with her handkerchief. She sniffed the air.

"Do you realize what a huge issue pets are for agents and

potential buyers?" she asked, her voice subdued, ominous.

"Our animals are all in their proper cages, Patty," Johanna said, and *her* eyes were wide with wonderment that anyone might express anything other than excitement at their collection.

"Do you realize how rightly concerned agents are about the way a pet-infested house will show and how the buyer will respond to it? Do you realize that buyers may be anxious to think that there are actually pets *in the home* at the time of viewing? Do you realize that buyers worry about what pets may have done to a home and especially how they've made it smell?"

"You cannot deprive buyers of any opportunity to see the space available..."

"Smell?" Johanna blanched.

"Don't you realize that most sellers cannot smell their own pets?"

"Patty," Nick pleaded. "Our animals are very clean. No one has ever complained and anyway, the buyers don't have to come into the menagerie. We'll just put a sign on the door that will say 'No entry during feeding hours' or something like that."

Patty shook her head gravely.

"You cannot deprive buyers of any opportunity to see the space available. How could they know how much *storage* might be behind those doors? Home owners afflicted with pets have many options but none of them is really acceptable."

"None?" Nick and Johanna whispered in unison.

"Every visible animal hair is a thousand dollars lost," Patty said, her eyes narrowing even more. "Every poo ten thousand. It's your money—or your pets."

"Even Big Jack and Little Annie?" Johanna wailed and I somehow knew she was referring to her pet donkeys. "What can we do with them?"

"There's only one solution," Patty confirmed. "And I believe it should be left to professionals. They're equipped to handle it quickly and painlessly."

Nick and Johanna had both put their hands to their mouths. Patty's attention was meanwhile drawn to a handsome, high-end baby carriage that was parked against the wall. She turned slowly back to the couple and for the first time I saw the ruddy glow behind her eyes.

"Do you have children?" she asked, her voice low.

"No!" Nick and Johanna shrieked. They backed away from her. "None! None!"

I never said you'd like me," Patty rumbled. Her voice and smile were terrible now. "I just said I'd get this place sold!"

But by then I was floating softly towards the ceiling. A gentle breeze was wafting me ever higher and I was looking down on the earnest sellers and their counselor from an ever greater height.

I heard another, reassuring voice from somewhere.

"A home has to look clean and inviting," the voice said. "But it must also have a personality of its own."

I realized it was the voice of Craig Pilgrim, the realtor, whom I'd just started to work with, the one who called me his secret weapon.

And then I was awake.

4.

Realtors and Reality

*It seemed to me that, whatever staging might be, it had
something to do with the world of real estate.*

ell, it couldn't be as stark as that, could it? Home staging couldn't be just the good works of the angel Stephanie, whom every home seller loved, or the terrible territory of the witch Patty, whose scorched-earth policies leveled everything before her. It was clear I had a lot to learn.

What actually was staging? Was it just something people did before the realtors held an open house? Was it something your neighbour, the one who wanted to be an interior designer, came in and did for you? Was it the sort of drama you saw on TV? Was it actually a profession, something people learned to do?

I set out to discover for myself and what follows is a series of conversations—my conversations with realtors and stagers with far more experience than I've had. That's been one of my ways of learning. I hope it will do the same for you.

It seemed to me that, whatever staging might be, it had something to do with the world of real estate. So where better to start than by talking with some realtors? I approached a few who gave me the equivalent of a snort. Why would they want anything to do with people who weren't even realtors themselves? What made a bunch of amateurs think they could sell houses better than professional realtors? Then my dad introduced me to Chona dela Cruz, who saw staging rather differently.

Chona dela Cruz

Chona dela Cruz: A Surprising Perspective

It seemed that my dreaming self had a pretty confident idea of what a house should offer prospective buyers who are just driving by. In fact I was confident enough that the Hargreaves appeared to have hung on my every word. But this book isn't just about house sellers and house buyers. It's also about the profession of house staging. And as we all know, if you're a professional, you get paid. House sellers have long been accustomed to paying real estate agents, who assist the sales process. How do people react to these new players, whom nobody had heard of twenty years ago?

I met with Chona dela Cruz at her Re/Max Elite office. Chona's been a residential realtor in Edmonton for almost eight years and as a family friend has proved sweetly supportive of my professional aspirations. I spoke with her for this book because I'd heard she was a realtor who believed in the effectiveness of professional staging. I thought she might have some answers—and was a bit surprised at the answers she did have.

"When I started in 2006," she told me, "eighty-thousand people were in the process of moving into Edmonton over just a couple of years. When you put a house up for sale, you'd get an average of thirteen offers or more. That's what's called a seller's market. Who needed staging? But today in Edmonton the residential housing market has stabilized—in fact I'd call it a buyer's market right now and that's one of the reasons selling tools such as home staging are becoming more and more a part of the picture, especially in the last three years."

"You personally think staging's effective, then?" I asked her.

"I personally believe in staging. I know a good stager can decorate a vacant house with tastefully chosen furniture and fittings and make it more appealing, but the real challenge is the staging of the occupied home because that's the majority of sellers and in fact it's actually easier to sell a vacant house than sell a cluttered, occupied house. That may sound strange but it's true. Seventy-five percent of my business originates with buyers and buyers are really turned off by clutter. Buyers want to see the floors, they want to see the counter tops. My buyers always pay close attention to the kitchen and a cluttered kitchen is a turn off for them.

But I think a professional stager can probably transform a cluttered, occupied house into a place that potential buyers feel good about. What stagers are after, whether they're approaching it from the direction of a vacant house or a cluttered occupied home, is the creation of a spacious but attractive space."

"So when you want to sell a house, you call in a stager."

"Well, not exactly. I myself supply the seller with a two-page list of things I want them to do. This is a list of basic home staging techniques that are all about working with what's there. The one I use is distributed by the real estate coaching firm, Buffini and Company. See, many of us realtors know staging works and what I'm trying to do is get the seller to pay attention to home-staging principles. The problem is that the occupants may love the house just the way it is and be quietly resistant to following those principles. That's why frankly it's helpful if the clients have paid a professional stager for that advice because people tend to take more seriously things they've paid for."

"So you see stagers as giving the seller the bad news about their houses?"

"There's truth in that. Some people just don't like to hear what we might need to tell them about their home and, you know, we realtors don't like to bear bad news. That's why ideally we'd love that part of the job to be done by staging professionals."

"So in theory there should be a ready role for home stagers."

"Yes, there are some strong arguments in favour of home staging, but I see its potential as far from fully developed. Many sellers still don't get it and are reluctant to pay for staging services on top of the fees and commissions already associated with selling a house. These other fees and commissions might average about fourteen thousand dollars here in Edmonton and that reluctance is why some realtors will actually step up themselves and engage the stager."

"The realtor is the client rather than the home seller?"

"I say *some* realtors."

"How many agents are there is your office?"

"I'm not sure exactly. Maybe one hundred and ten. Certainly more than one hundred."

"So how many of those use stagers."

"Well, I'm just estimating. Maybe five."

"Five?"

"Something like that. I suppose the others, they're worried about the extra cost. I personally try to convince sellers of the merits of staging—which I believe in—but I want to make sure I've got a motivated seller first. If a seller is only testing the market or for any other reason is not fully motivated, a realtor won't want to commit to the extra expense either."

"I'm really amazed, Chona, that if something is as effective as you describe home staging to be, only five percent of realtors will employ them."

"It's not just the realtors. There's another factor too. I've been approached by many people wanting to act as home stagers. I normally ask for them to send me a brochure describing their service but—and this is surprising—almost none have done so. We get brochures from electricians and home inspectors and other related trades—but not stagers. They just seem to disappear. So another factor in the relatively scant use of staging services is the fact that the field in full of people who are untrained and, you know, unprofessional. Such people become quickly discouraged. Demand for the service is still relatively small so the effect is circular: few people successfully enter the field. Maybe one of the missing ingredients is the capital necessary to brand their services."

"So does the real estate business need stagers or not?"

"*I* think so. I'm hoping that the staging business evolves here to the point where we've got a number—a limited number—of professional stagers who have the experience and reputations that will make them a reliable resource, the sort of resource that sellers and realtors will be happy to invest in. This is the challenge I put out to sellers: If you really want to sell your house, are you willing to keep it on the market for months, cleaning the place every time somebody wants to see it? Or would you be willing to pay a reasonable fee to a professional stager and work with them? Remember, a well-staged home normally sells in less that thirty days. That would be my challenge to sellers—and to us realtors too."

I was really struck that this experienced realtor described a valuable service as a challenge to those who used it.

"So then, would you use stagers, Chona?"

"Yes, I would."

"Are you using them now?

"No."

"Have you ever used one?"

"No."

I thought about this for a moment.

"Wow. Why not?"

"Well, one reason is that many of my properties have multiple occupants. They'd dismantle a staging job the first afternoon. But there's something more important for me. Professional stagers charge professional fees. I'm an agent working on commission and I work hard. I'm not prepared at this point to pay for yet another service, especially when many clients are just testing the waters. That's goes for me and a lot of agents like me."

"But if you had the right client, you'd consider a stager?"

"Stephanie, my dear, I'll call you when I need a stager."

Well, that was nice, so we said good-bye and I went home thinking about Chona's remarkable candour. She believed staging to be of great value and would employ a stager but never has.

Hmm.

Craig Pilgrim: Showing It Like It Is

Craig Pilgrim

Remember how, in my first dream, James noticed the pile of old sneakers in his front entranceway? That was his first glimpse of his house from a buyer's perspective. Remember how the demon stager Patty *only* saw the house from the buyer's perspective—and she didn't like what she saw?

"Clutter" is a word you hear a lot in discussions of home staging. It's clearly bad news— not as bad as "mice" and "urine" and "bedbugs"—but bad. For many people writing about staging, getting rid of clutter seems to be what it's all about. We picture eager stagers backing a dumpster up to the front door and hiring a crew with wheelbarrows to empty out the clutter—*all* of it.

But wait. If we look a little closer, we see clutter represents a more nuanced idea. There are very few of us who are not attached to our possessions, and because our houses are fixed in location, these possessions tend to accumulate. Some may belong with the imitation cloisonné Aunt Ellen brought back from Hong Kong—they're there because they have to be—but most are there because we like them. They are part of our lives, the familiar accessories that enrichen our surroundings. So is that what clutter is? The things we love?

As you'll see from my conversations, there appears at first to be some disagreement on this subject. Chona dela Cruz's long experience as a realtor has convinced her that "in fact it's actually easier to sell a vacant house than sell a cluttered occupied house." Chona has sold more than a few houses in her career and, based on her observations alone, I might have been prepared to strip a house bare as the first step. However in the course of my on-going investigation of staging, I had come across Craig Pilgrim.

I live and work in Edmonton, a rapidly growing city where a lot of the housing stock is just fifteen or twenty years old. Although the clay subsoil can lead to structural problems, these are not usually serious. True decrepitude, in other words, is only rarely an issue in Edmonton and how a house presents aesthetically is often the most important factor from a staging and selling perspective.

Early on in my inquiries I had ample opportunity to talk to one of the more active realtors in the greater Edmonton area. Craig Pilgrim at Re/Max is a member of the Realtors Association of Edmonton®, the Alberta Real Estate Association, and the Canadian Real Estate Association. He's also a terrifically good-humoured, light-hearted guy who's just fun to talk to. He's been licensed for nine years now and he and I have had occasion to work together as I started into staging. I knew he had thoughts on staging and I knew these thoughts were often at odds with certain popular views.

"Staging?" he said, when I raised the subject. "I never thought about such a thing when I was first in the real estate business. But I started to change my mind as I became more experienced and by four or five years ago it was a regular part of my business. I could see there were clearly two types of staging—the staging of vacant houses and the staging of occupied homes—and I saw they'd require different approaches. Maybe thirty percent of the houses on the Edmonton market are vacant. Dressing these shells up to look warm, inviting and occupied is where the staging craft overlaps with interior decoration. This of course is going to cost money—maybe two thousand dollars a month. It's an advantage if it's done right but not everybody is prepared to make the commitment."

"Another realtor I spoke to told me these empty places were actually easier to sell than an occupied house."

"Well, in some respects you can see how that might be, though I'd never leave a house totally bare if I had the choice. But the fact is, most homes for sale are occupied and in these cases, I'm saying one hundred percent require staging treatment of some sort, even if it's just a basic consult. I've never met a seller who wouldn't benefit from staging but it's not just the sellers who stand to benefit. The realtor benefits too because one of the things we like doing least is telling our selling clients that something about their home is undesirable. If I can shift this important part of the process to the staging consultant, that goes far to improve my relationship with my client."

"Right," I laughed. "That's one of the things we're here for. But I wanted to talk to you about clutter."

"Clutter?"

"The great killer of house sales."

Craig frowned. "Oh, right. Clutter. Well, first, the point everyone agrees on. We set up our homes to please ourselves and we're not all alike. Sometimes we make choices that reflect some unusual aspect of ourselves that may not sit well with most others. So the first act of staging is to remove objects that may actually *harm* a sale."

"Of course," I said. "Depersonalize. You hear that all the time. But as a new staging consultant, I think one of my most important roles is to be sensitive, not just to the buyer's wishes, but to the feelings of the sellers, the people who actually still live in this house. It would be hard to tell people their world is just so much...*clutter.*"

Craig snorted. "I can't believe the kinda nonsense people watch on TLC and HGTV. The stagers are supposed to come in and knock out walls and rip up floors and laugh at the owners. People live in their homes and despite what they tell you on HGTV, buyers know this. They're not stupid. They can tell when a place is heavily staged. It's not realistic and in my experience it turns buyers off. They say, "Who lives like this?" I know there are people who disagree, but I'm basing this on my own experience. What are they doing, denuding the fridge, stripping off the kid's drawings and so on? Don't you want people to come into a million-dollar home and say, 'Wow! We can have a million-dollar home and kids too!' And all that stuff about pets killing sales. What are people supposed to do, send their pets to the pound? Obviously, staging means eliminating offensive smells and in-your-face evidence of untrained animals, but a positive message is, 'This house is pet-friendly.' Why? Because most people own pets. I'm for real-life staging."

"So you're *for* clutter, Craig?"

"No. It's all about balance. A talented stager will help the clients/sellers distinguish between what's a real part of their daily lives and what's clutter. This kind of stager knows enough to ask the client if they might have blue towels. Well, yes, they do, and the stager can explain how using them in this room will enhance the overall effect. Buyers come to the house and they don't think 'staged.' They think, 'This house looks lived in and it looks good too.'"

"So they'd respond to it better than to, say, a model home?"
Craig rolls his eyes.

"Those model homes you see in new developments and at building shows? What do they say to you? They say 'look—don't touch' and buyers know when a place sends the 'look—don't touch' message of a model home. They recognize artificiality when they see it. Who wants to buy artificial? You want to sell artificial?

"As you know, Stephanie, these are just the sorts of

You know how set designers can take a film set and make it look like real people live there? That's what a real stager can do with an empty house.

things I talk to my clients about before I bring someone like you in for a consultation. I make sure they're aware that I believe a home has to look inviting but it has to have a personality of its own and those two things together are why I'm recommending a stager. And by the way, when we're selling a vacant home and I or the seller call in a stager to furnish it, I expect to see an interior that the prospective buyers can't initially distinguish from an actual occupied home. I don't want to see a 'model home.' You know how set designers can take a film set and make it look like real people live there? That's what a real stager can do with an empty house. They don't call them 'stagers' for nothing. Their job is to put life onto a space, not take the life out of it. Why? Because that's what buyers—and sellers too—respond to."

"Wow. You hear the opposite pretty often."

"Yeah, you do. I'm sorry to say that too many people

striving to work as stagers think it's okay to strip a place bare and put in a few accent pillows and an artsy-fartsy vase or two—as though that 'magic' is going to sell the house. Nonsense. I think some stagers must be learning this at staging school. Or they're watching too many reality shows about real estate. Listen, a lot of reality TV is about destruction and humiliation. Some people may find that funny to watch but it's no template for how to sell a real house. And if a few misguided stagers think making the seller feel bad makes them feel good, well, if it doesn't sell the house, what good is it really?"

...a few misguided stagers think making the seller feel bad makes them feel good...

"You make it sound obvious. Funny how sterility is a sort of ideal."

"I think this distorted idea about staging is partly the fault of the realtor profession, that is, some members of it. These people unfortunately believe in a 'turnstile' model of selling houses. They believe in 'get it in and get it gone' rather than providing the service needed to deliver real value to everyone involved. These are the 'quantity' people rather than the 'quality' people. There's also those who don't know better, but let's not talk about them."

"Actually, Craig, I know a stager here in town who I think's really good, and she completely altered the interior."

"Where was it?"

"Glenora."

"Okay. Glenora. There are of course exceptions. In Edmonton the housing stock is pretty new but we do have a few older neighbourhoods that are addresses of prestige and much sought after. In these cases, a stager might sometimes opt for the more extreme approach. Maybe the occupants might move out and the stager might want to avoid the personal approach but in those cases we're looking for a completely different kind of buyer. Maybe sixteen or seventeen hundred trades per month go through the Edmonton Real Estate Board. The vast majority of these are average buyers and average sellers with ordinary motivations. And in those everyday situations, I stick by my philosophy: staging is invaluable but it's not about radical transformation or the elimination of the seller's personality."

Okay. So maybe it wasn't a simple matter of depersonalizing. Maybe the philosophy of staging rested on some other basis. If so, I felt I had to understand more about the staging business rather than the staging craft. And I knew who to talk to.

5.

Staging Minds

When a home is up for sale, should it be stripped of visible signs of the owner's personality, or should that personality be allowed to show through?

Staging is a developing profession whose role in the world of real estate is only now starting to be felt. Young stagers like me are striving to understand what experienced colleagues are doing to improve the effectiveness of real estate transactions. In this regard, nothing has proven a more powerful tool that the MasterMind groups.

In 1937, Napoleon Hill wrote a book he called *Think and Grow Rich*, in which he defined the mastermind as a "coordination of knowledge and effort, in a spirit of harmony, between two or more people, for the attainment of a definite purpose." Hill claimed to have been inspired by the great steel tycoon Andrew Carnegie, who established a mastermind group that consisted of "a staff of approximately fifty men, with whom he surrounded himself, for the *definite purpose* of manufacturing and marketing steel. He attributed his entire fortune to the *power* he accumulated through this *Master Mind*. Since Hill, MasterMind groups have proliferated and are today a staple tool of numerous successful people. A half dozen of us put a MasterMind group of stagers together under the leadership of our mentor, Karen Schaefer. We had our first meeting in San Diego in February, 2013.

The fundamental MasterMind principle is that of sharing—the sharing of knowledge and experience. I'm going to introduce you to several members of this group, talented designers and successful entrepreneurs whose wealth of professional wisdom has been so helpful to me.

Karen Schaefer: Making Professionals

I guess it's not surprising that some of my best insights into the world of staging have come from the warm, caring person who is my personal mentor and guide.

Some ten years ago, when Karen Schaefer and her husband found themselves in challenging financial circumstances, Karen attended a seminar on real-estate investing. "If these people can do it," she thought, "so can I." She borrowed to finance her further education in the field and borrowed to buy a number of houses.

"Now," she wondered, "What can I do to make these places sell—and fast?" and turned quite naturally to her earlier acting and film career.

"I thought I'd do what I could to make the interiors look like movie sets. I knew the magic of movies and I knew movie-makers depended for that magic on the creation of scenes. But to know how to do that, you had to know what the scene was about and who it was for. I knew nothing formally about staging—I didn't even know staging was a profession—but I followed my instincts. Actually, I took the furniture out of our own home and used it to decorate the one I was selling at the time. My poor husband claims he'd come home at night and fall on the floor because I'd taken his chair.

"My houses were selling and soon other real estate investors like myself were coming to me and saying, 'Hey, how did you do that?' I began to do my thing for them, in the houses they had for sale."

"So that's how you became a home-staging trainer?"

"No no. I didn't connect the dots at all. But one day I was approached by a gentleman running the local real estate investors group. He came up to me and said, 'Have you ever thought about teaching this?'

"'Teaching what?' I asked him.

"'Teaching people how to make their houses sell,'" he said.

Going for It

There can be no doubt about it: the kitchen of a modern home is what sells it. The type of kitchen that appears in this photo is the type that appears in many homes. It works satisfactorily and the owners have adapted to it. But in the kitchen as nowhere else, buyers want new, they want style, and they want luxury.

New cupboards and counters are a not-inconsiderable investment for the seller. But this is not an investment that will be overlooked by potential buyers. And when a kitchen is thoroughly updated, the final effect can be created even in a small space through the use of very few items—provided, as Karen teaches, that the stager follows the concepts of colour, continuity, theme and flow. Here, the red accents tie everything together and make it welcoming.

Under the guidance of her new mentor, Karen systemized her approach into six simple steps and wrote her first book on staging—for real estate investors. She worked as a stager herself for about a year but was soon employing her old public speaking skills to spread the word to others, including to home decorators. Today she operates her training program in fourteen countries from her head office in Colorado Springs.

I talked to her at one of the MasterMind seminars she conducts for our group.

"While this was going on," she told me, "I became increasingly interested in marketing and came to understand that the foundations of business of any type are effective strategies and creative marketing concepts. That's why the stagers I've trained are among the most successful in the world. We're talking about evolving from amateurism to professionalism."

When you talk to Karen, if you know she's a staging trainer but don't know her background, you'd expect the whole conversation to be about staging techniques—and she is in fact a master of these. But her specialty is not arranging lighting and moving furniture, but rather the *business* of staging. The blunt truth is that most people entering the staging field are stronger in staging skills than in business skills and this explains why the staging world sometimes seems populated by talented amateurs. These women—there are male stagers but not many at this point—love working with interiors but don't understand enough about the financial realities of the field to make a true living. They may in fact not have the aptitude or taste for business and this has repercussions for them and for their clients. I would see this sharply illustrated when I later interviewed staging entrepreneur Kristy Morrison, a member of our MasterMind group who certainly does have the aptitude.

"I'm not saying everyone who enters the field should aim to be an employee," Karen told me. "Actually, I think everyone should try to learn the basics of running their own business. But it's a fact that not everyone will follow this path."

Of course she knew that running my own business was a personal ambition.

"And I expect you to succeed," she laughed.

"I expect that too," I said. "But I have to say that a big part of the successful staging business is our relationship with realtors. I think that's a real challenge for new entrants to staging. I feel I've been lucky in that regard."

"There are a lot of good realtors out there who know the value of staging a home," Karen said. "They know that a well-staged home will sell for significantly more than an unstaged or ineffectively staged one. The problem realtors face is not that they don't get it, it's that they often find it difficult to sell it to clients."

I thought about Chona, who'd described that very thing.

*Here, in a very different and much older home, Karen recognized a room
with tons of potential. The fireplace has great detail but is a bit lost
because the white provides no contrast with the walls.*

Karen is a great believer in economy of staging. With an absolute minimum of small accessories, she has accented the fireplace in this room, one of its best features. The vases balance it out and the globe brings the eye down to the casing at the base.

"But that's where a first-class stager will step in and say, 'You don't have to sell staging to your client. That's my job. Just introduce me to your seller.' That's why a first-class stager doesn't just work with realtors. They're able to work directly with real estate investors too. In fact, a lot of our training focuses on investors, because they're people who repeatedly offer houses for sale. My advice to new stagers is—don't put all your eggs in one basket. Get to know both realtors and real-estate investors. The investor is there for that "smelly" house that no one wants except the investor—because he can smell the money. Learning to stage houses for this sort of market can be lucrative for stagers, because they're quick in-and-out jobs that don't require extensive furnishings.

"In fact, contrary to popular belief, a good stager doesn't need a whole lot of either. Build relationships with two highly productive agents and two highly productive real estate investors. They'll appreciate your contribution to their business, they'll appreciate your savvy, your being able to communicate with the client, your ability to get into and out of the property quickly. They'll come to rely upon your professionalism.

"So even though the statistics prove that staging works, stagers may never convince ninety-five percent of agents to use their services. What I'm saying is, stagers don't need that ninety-five percent. They need the five percent who do most of the work, get most of the results and are in fact the most receptive to staging as a tool."

We turned to the philosophy of staging and we had a chuckle about my dreams. What, I wondered, was her view. When a home is up for sale, should it be stripped of visible signs of the owner's personality, or should that personality be allowed to show through? Karen was thoroughly familiar with this seeming contradiction.

"Staging has been around since the 1970s. I myself have been active in the field for about eight years. What we see is that ideas about what constitutes good staging change in the same way that fashions change. Old tricks like baking bread, for example, become familiar and aren't effective past a certain point. That's true today of depersonalizing. We're nosy as a society now and we want to see more of how people live. As a result, these older tactics must give way to something new.

"But all this is looking at staging from the point of view of taste, but in fact, staging should never be allowed to come down to issues of taste. Staging is about what makes the property sell. That is the difference between staging and decorating. What needs to be done to this particular house to make it sell effectively? If the solution is stripping it of the owner's personality, then that's the best staging. If the

The bars on this window make the room very uninviting, don't you think? Karen thought so, but the owner wouldn't remove the bars or allow window dressings. Her solution? "You have to give the buyer something else to fall in love with so these things don't matter."

With her signature minimalism, Karen provides pillows and teacups that sug-
gest someone (especially me) sitting there and reading or relaxing and enjoying
a warm summer day. And lo and behold—you barely see those bars.

solution is retaining the owner's furniture and décor and kids' drawings, that's the best staging.

"Our job is to figure out who is likely to buy this house and cause them to fall in love with it. We're looking to create a 'pocket of emotion' that will differentiate this house from any other. As potential buyers go on to look at twenty-five other places, we want them to think back and say, 'Yeah, but what about that house that had the...' "

I myself am a young person just entering the profession. I haven't met that many people like myself. I asked Karen who she thought was the typical stager.

"The average person going into staging is a fifty-something woman, either on a second career or a 'it's my time' person who has devoted many years to, say, raising children. It's her time now. Of course many of these people may be part-timers and not all will set standards as high as they should. That's part of what our training is about: setting standards and making it relatively easy for new stagers to follow them.

"Of course there are training firms that don't do that. There are fly-by-night stagers and fly-by-night trainers. But these allow the serious people to better differentiate themselves. The people who aren't serious will just go away by themselves."

"Our trainees often arrive with misconceptions. Two types of stagers come to us. The first is someone for whom staging

It's transformed! The pieces of patio furniture under the trees tie them to the house and suggest a leisurely lifestyle. The painted deck furniture and the deck itself draw your eye towards the entrance. The general clean-up, the paint, the flowers at the entrance—even the beginnings of a tended lawn—all invite us to come in.

want?' Improperly trained and/or fly-by-night stagers might be decorating, but staging has a different goal altogether: it's ultimately the art of selling. An improperly trained stager doesn't know how to assess the potential buyers for a given property. They don't know who they're staging for. An improperly trained stager doesn't grasp how to create true flow in a home, flow that guides the viewer through, showing off the best features first and last. An improperly trained stager may not even appreciate that it is in fact possible to influence a buyer's path through a property."

"Well, Karen, now you've brought up the subject, I have to ask you about actual techniques of staging. I know these may change with time but everyone's still very interested in how it's properly done by real professionals."

Karen laughed.

"So you want to know if we can be tricky, right? Well, we can, but in the best way possible.

"We train stagers in many skills, but this influencing the visitor's flow path through the home is an example of a more advanced set of skills. For example, we break a house into quadrants and try to guide viewers through those quadrants in the most favourable way. When visitors enter the home, we like them to 'own' it. We'll sometimes set up a large mirror so that they see themselves in the home from the first moment. We use what we call 'leaders'—perhaps nothing more than a nicely framed welcome message and a table with offerings of sparkling water. These leaders draw viewers forward in a certain direction. On the other hand, we may place our 'stoppers' along the way to steer viewers away from a path that might cause them to miss a good feature or approach a room from a less than optimal direction. These kind of artful techniques are only a small sample of a professional stager's repertory of skills, but they're all a part of what we believe to be the stager's ultimate job: to create the experience that the buyer is looking for. Making a home beautiful and engaging and interactive and enjoyable are actually critical components of the stager's job and stagers who don't understand that are doing a disservice to their clients and themselves."

"I was talking to Craig Pilgrim, a realtor in Edmonton. Craig's a believer in staging but also a believer in letting the seller's personality show through. I'd call him an advocate of restrained staging. When we were talking he mentioned how staging high-end homes can require quite different techniques. I know that when you personally engage in staging, you often tackle high-end properties. Can you tell me how they might be different."

"Stephanie, you're a trained stager at this point. You know all staging has the same goal: to sell the house, not beautify it or strip it of its character. But occupied high-end homes, when they come on the market, do present different challenges. For one thing, they're most often already beautifully appointed. They probably have the twenty-thousand-dollar sofa that was chosen by a professional designer, and the carpets, lamps, chairs, tables, appliances and fixtures that are of equivalent quality. A stager isn't likely to have that sort of thing in stock or even be able to rent it. And in many cases, affluent homes are highly customized, with features that are important to the seller and that you as the stager can't just eliminate but must work with. The affluent seller will often be very forthright in telling a stager when they think some change won't work. For these reasons the stager who takes on the challenge of an affluent home must be more than usually prepared to understand the mindset not only of the potential buyer but also of the seller. It's just a more dramatic example of how a good stager is sensitive to sellers while trying to serve their best interests."

Alright. So it wasn't so much a question of whether to depersonalize a home or show it warts and all. And it wasn't a question of whether to bake cookies for a viewing or send the dogs to a kennel. All these factors can vary with fashion and circumstance. But as Karen sees it, the eternal truth of the staging professional is the obligation to sell the house quickly and for the best price possible—from the seller's perspective.

Kristy Morrison: A Stagers' Stager

I was fascinated to see how this nuts-and-bolts business-like attitude might resolve the seeming "philosophical" question of the right approach to a staging assignment. Of course there was still the problem of how to sell the house best. That remained the mysterious "secret" of the profession.

The subject of the business-like approach, though, was at the forefront when I went to see Kristy Morrison in Ottawa. This is an exceptionally vital, personable and humourous person who puts you at ease pretty quickly.

"I'd been a veterinary technician and my husband and I were doing pretty well. We had a couple of houses, a couple of jobs, a couple of mortgages. Then Eric lost his job when his company downsized. He'd just found a new one when-you guessed it-I lost mine."

Just as had happened to her mentor (and mine), Karen Schaefer in California, the couple found themselves in difficult circumstances, overextended to the tune of two

It's rare that a stager gets to cut their teeth on their own house, but this is the one Kristy describes in my interview with her.

The home sat for six months in a strong sellers' market because the whole place was purple: the carpet, the walls, the ceiling, baseboards, even the custom light switches Buyers couldn't see past the décor and Kristy finally bought it for

$10,000 off the list price. She and her husband lived there for four years.

This is the living room and the purple colour is a time machine that takes us back and back. The room appears small and its purpose uncertain. Buyers can't see past this sort of effect and Kristy's purchase isn't the first eccentrically decorated home to sit on the market for a very long time.

"We painted the whole place," Kristy told me, "and with the new kitchen and new flooring and lighting, we invested about 10,000 dollars and a lot of work."

The overall effect here is somehow dismal, almost depressing despite the window. The purply walls and the carpet blend together to create a monotone—and not in a nice way. The furniture is of another era and the candelabra, although it might look pleasant at night, can't provide anything otherwise.

The dining room certainly needed a lot of work and Kristy focused on the key elements. She painted the walls a neutral colour that would attract a larger percentage of buyers, then painted a feature wall a rich colour that defines the room. The mirror on the feature wall makes the room look bigger. Replacing the purple carpet with hardwood flooring not only solved a potential health and sanitation issue, but created a floor a whole lot easier to clean. To say nothing of actually beautiful.

houses. Kristy was considering going back to clinical work.

"The first house was, well, a bit, um, sticky. It was painted horrible colours—I'd bought it that way—and I'd never had a chance to change it. I had to get rid of it because of the commute to a new job but it sat on the market for a year and a half before it sold.

"Eventually the second house had to go too and I brought in a real estate agent. 'You're going to sit for at least six months,' he told us. 'That's the current state of market saturation in your area. There are plenty of houses directly comparable to yours.'

"But by then I'd started to take a home staging course from Karen Schaefer and decided I'd apply its principles throughout the second place. This was a fairly recently built bungalow in the country, but its finish and condition made it look older. The living room had been painted with a nasty high-gloss canary yellow Venetian plaster and the other rooms each had their own scheme. It was pretty horrible.

"We streamlined the interior by painting neutral colours throughout and opening up the basement. We re-laid the floors with hardwood instead of ninety-nine-cent laminate. I added my accessories. We didn't go all the way—we didn't put in a new kitchen, for example—but everything we did was clean and organized and by now I understood that this sort of careful investment could be well repaid. We put the house up for sale and it went for full price within four hours of listing."

That was how Kristy entered the home staging profession but knowing what she does today, I was a bit puzzled.

"I guess you saw yourself as starting a typical single-person service business," I prompted her. "I mean, I guess you were totally devoted to staging houses."

"No. That's just it. I saw my role differently even before I began. I researched the business and I realized it was filled with people working part time. 'Don't even bother getting into it,' one stager said. 'You'll never be successful.' Believe me, that's what lit my fire. I saw right off that almost nobody in the business hired anyone else. There were no jobs, just isolated entrepreneurs. And I also saw that staging skills were very different from business skills. They're two different sides of the mind. A lot of people were going out of business who were really good at staging but couldn't handle the business side. So right from the start I saw my role as an executive organizer who would actually hire stagers and give them jobs. I set up the systems and procedures necessary to make a business work. My stagers weren't like real estate brokers, who are independent contractors. The people on my team are actually staff and follow our company procedures: when they go into a consultation, they always do a presentation, they always use our detailed home evaluation handbook, they always have to sit down with the home owner and talk about our overall suggestions and they always have to do a follow-up report to keep the real estate

This kitchen needed serious work. The wall paper, the brick, the cabinets: all are dated and the mixture of colors weigh down the room. Investment in kitchen upgrades are seldom cheap but always have a profound effect on a house.

The dark cabinets don't just modernize this room, they enrich it. The updated brick around the window creates a focal point and the backsplash ties the room together while the soft touches of red accents have helped make this house a home.

Kristy did a lot more here than a typical staging job because she was actually upgrading her own house. But the principles as she applied them will work for even a modest staging upgrade.

Same house. A room with a fireplace and a large window has a lot of potential but the clunky décor must have been very off-putting for buyers.

Obviously Kristy's transformation took a lot of time and hard work. The addition of the brick around the fireplace created a textured focal point that draws buyers' eyes to the fireplace feature. The bookcases give the room more storage and purpose...and as we all know, storage is important. The dark wood flooring and the neutral walls look perfect together. The furniture is perfectly to scale and the upholsterypattern is neither overly bold nor dull.

agent in the loop. This consistency means that a realtor can recommend our firm by name, knowing that whoever takes the assignment is going to deliver.

"The beauty of this system for many talented stagers is that they don't have to worry about the daunting challenge of running a business: networking, complications in negotiations with clients, marketing, presentations, accounting and on and on. My staff consists of great stagers who found they couldn't run an independent business, but some of them are probably better at staging than I am."

"When you say 'networking,' who do you mean?"

"Real estate agents."

"But I've got the impression that few realtors actually use stagers."

"That's right. The eighty/twenty rule applies to agents: twenty percent do eighty percent of the work. The really productive minority of realtors are almost all working with stagers. On the other hand, home owners who try to sell their own homes rarely use stagers because they see their houses as perfect already. And the less productive realtors rarely use stagers because they're terrified of offending the owner and losing one of their few listings. You can talk to these two groups until you're blue in the face about how staging shortens the time the house will be sitting on the market, how they're improving on their investment, how they're reducing the number of low-ball offers. You can talk but they can't hear. It's a steep and expensive learning curve for them."

"Expensive because—?"

"Expensive because knocking off your house price is like losing twenty-thousand dollars down a grate in the sidewalk. Mind you, ask those realtors and they'll tell you staging is a wonderful, effective tool. Then suggest an appointment to meet. 'Um, not now,' they'll say. 'I can't afford it at the moment'"

"So for these agents staging doesn't look like a cost of doing business."

Kristy has an infectious laugh and she's laughing at this point.

"Know what really boggles me? Realtors who spend one hundred and fifty dollars—maybe three hundred dollars—on professional photographs of an unstaged home. Wow! What a horrible idea!"

Shortly after Kristy launched her business, she became a member of the Real Estate Staging Association (RESA), based out of Valley Springs, California. But at the same time she was listening to her fellow stagers and what she heard were people who wanted contact with other staging professionals in the Ottawa area. She went out and found a location and invited other RESA members to form a local chapter. Soon they were inviting local non-RESA stagers to join. This was clearly the same impulse—working with peers—that was the basis of Kristy's own business.

"It also had the effect of strengthening the profession locally. To that point, there had been no coherent fee structure in the Ottawa area staging business. Stagers still suffered from a false sense of rivalry. Often, when I'd call a stager, she'd fail to return my call. I thought about how chilling that must be for people just entering the field."

"I'm sure many of them thought of it as a terribly competitive profession."

"Right. But look, my company is pretty organized and productive. Last year we did four hundred stagings. Think that's a lot? Last year there were fourteen thousand houses sold by real estate agents in the Ottawa area. That's not including the builder market, the property management market or the for-sale-by-owner market. I train stagers, as you know. People say to me, 'Why would you be creating your own competition?' But I don't see them as competition. The market's too huge. Also, I know the mentality of many people entering staging and I know many of them will only want to do it part-time. This wouldn't be true competition under any normal market conditions."

My discussion with Kristy had painted a picture of staging as a profession faced at present with almost boundless opportunity. Houses are always going to be sold. They sell better if they're carefully prepared to receive viewers. This requires professional skills and resources. Few transactions are taking advantage of this tool, but here was someone so optimistic about the future of staging, she was prepared to build a business based on employing other stagers and training even more of them. What opinions, I wondered, would such a person hold about the "theory" of staging? I had the impression that the experience of plenty of stagers had convinced them that the personality of the owner/seller was an impediment for the average buyer. And then there were people like realtor Craig Pilgrim, who was convinced that the radical modification and neutralizing of an occupied house was nonsense perpetuated by the likes of HGTV?

Kristy was perfectly familiar with this controversy.

"In our business, when we're dealing with a re-sale home—one that's occupied as opposed to a new build—we focus more on keeping the personality of the seller/owner. We just can't sell them as model homes any more. And there's a sound, emotionally-based reason for that. We set up a house like a model home, people come in and say, 'Wow. Yeah. Really attractive, but my family would destroy this in thirty seconds. Let's move on to the next one.' They just can't connect emotionally. It looks like a house they'd see on TV. We need people to come in and say, 'This makes sense. This would be the place for me, my kids, my dogs. I can relate to this place.' Think of when you go over to a friend's perfect home and you've got your two-year-old with you. You're so afraid your child is going to disturb the perfection, you can't

Small is Beautiful

Finally, just a single example of Kristy's staging of a condo.

X

"This was a small two-bedroom penthouse unit about eight hundred square feet," she explains. "Since it was so small, buyers needed furniture to understand the layout. They understood and they bought."

relax and enjoy the visit. It's the same thing. The viewer pictures her two-year-old hitting his head on the corner of the chic glass table and sort of shudders inside.

"Don't misunderstand me. I'm not talking about leaving the house in everyday condition with laundry piled on the floor and family pictures in every single room. But I am talking about leaving emotional evidence of the occupying family that will allow the viewer to connect. Of course we keep our target buyer in mind, but if this is, say, a starter home, we might leave the seller's wedding photos in the living room. We'll leave the family's games in the family room. We'll leave the baby's things in the nursery room. Those are the hooks that allow a sense of emotional connection.

"The way staging used to be, stagers really did create model homes. They'd remove absolutely everything—the owner's horrible couches, their horrible décor, their horrible photos—and bring in a whole new interior. Believe me, that doesn't work anymore, not in Ottawa anyway. It flat out isn't happening. Even if I'm staging a brand-new build—no one lives there—I'll bring in my own wedding photos and other stuff that suggests a particular person lives there. Yes, it will be in some respects a 'model home,' but it will still contain highly personal elements."

I was beginning to see that there wasn't perhaps as much disagreement between stagers as had appeared. Some thought about staged houses as 'model' homes to which they added some personal elements. Others thought of staged homes as the real dwelling places of real occupants, but places that had to be carefully tidied and thoughtfully arranged so as not to put off buyers.

"Absolutely," Kristy said. "It's all about balance."

Carla Woolnough: The Case for Depersonalization

arla Woolnough is a respected member of our Master-Mind group, a former student of Karen Schaefer, and president of Nex-Step Design in Guelph, Ontario. Carla's dad has been in real estate most of his life so perhaps it wasn't surprising when Carla, with her flair for design, discovered home staging some eight years ago. At the time, the first staging pioneers had only been active for a few years. She's may be the quietest of our group—perhaps even a bit inscrutable—and a terrific stager.

In the kitchen of that same home Carla reminds us that kitchens are one of the main "selling rooms." We wanted to make sure that this one wowed buyers. All the stuff on the counters and floor made the space feel cramped and dated—not a place where buyers would feel comfortable cooking meals for family and friends."

Kitchen's—where families meet for a meal after a busy day at school or work—are indeed the heart of a home. We can learn something valuable about staging here. It's well lived in, and many prospective buyers would have the kitchen looking like this within a few months. But to show it exactly as the owner lives in it somehow takes away from the magic.

Carla worked with a limited budget, doing simple things like repainting the walls and cabinets and replacing the counter. That was enough to completely change the appearance of the kitchen. By leaving only a few key items on the counter she was able to convey how much counter space there really was.

"It was a lot more difficult then," she told me. "Very few people knew what we were talking about and in fact the level of awareness of staging is one of the things that has changed the most since I began. A lot of this can be put down to HGTV, which devoted so much attention to staging at one point and really educated realtors and the public as to the role of staging. Then the social media emerged on line and realtors who understood this new tool could see what buyers really wanted. At the same time, more people were joining the staging profession, and of course they helped to increase general awareness. That awareness is the biggest development since I began.

"Of course there are still plenty of old-school realtors who resist the idea of staging. They developed their way of working at a time when buyers were willing pay top dollars for a house that still needed work. The realtor would just say to the seller, "Now, don't forget to tidy the house and, oh, you better rake the lawn, okay?" That's no longer the case. Buyers have changed. They want to spend their money on a house that needs absolutely nothing done. A new generation of realtors knows that. They know their reputation depends on getting houses sold—and quickly. And gradually the old school realtors are beginning to come around too. They're starting to realize that if they want to stay competitive, they've got to listen to the buyers, not just the sellers. They're starting to understand that staging is part of their marketing, not just some frill. It costs money when a house doesn't sell during the first round. In many ways, staging is no different from photography. Nobody is so old-school, they'd dismiss the value of a good photograph. If a realtor couldn't be bothered paying for proper photographs and stuck up something on the agency's website that she'd shot herself, with the wrong lenses and bad lighting, she'd suffer, because the first place prospective buyers look is on-line.

"These tools—photography and staging and advertising and others—are part of the cost of selling. Sure, there are still plenty of sellers who can't grasp the concept of spending money on staging to sell their house, but those sellers aren't the future for realtors—and with time all sellers will become better educated about the benefits—the necessity—of staging."

I mentioned to Carla how Chona dela Cruz, the Edmonton realtor, had observed that only perhaps five realtors out of the hundred-odd at her agency actually used stagers. That didn't seemed like much penetration of the market, even if, as Kristy had suggested twentypercent did eightypercent of the work. I asked Carla about her own experience.

"Realistically," she said, "it *is* about five percent. And eight years ago, when I started it was—who knows?—one percent?" She laughed. "We've come a long way since then. At least now realtors *know* they need education."

So it was time to bring up my favorite problem: the

This home had been well lived in and needed a lot of work throughout," Carla said. "The family room had an amazing view of the backyard, but it was so stuffed with furniture, you didn't even notice the bay window, the fireplace, the hardwood floors."

The fact that the furniture was oversized made the room look small and limited. Furniture complements a room when it's to scale. This room looks very cold, red's and bright tones would help accent the nice wood flooring hiding under the rug.

The sellers were on a limited budget so we had to work with what they had, but by adding slipcovers to the old sofa and chair, and by removing about half the contents, buyers could see the great features of the room."

Amazing job. The slip covers kept the cost low for the sellers, yet created an effective space that would appeal to anyone. Carla reported that this home sold in three weeks for 3000.00 dollars over list.

"philosophy" of staging. I told Carla how Craig Pilgrim had expressed himself in no uncertain terms: he didn't like to see a home stripped of its occupants' personalities. Craig is a strong advocate of staging but he sees it as a careful adjustment of the home's existing personal elements. His own preference is for allowing the "lived in" quality to shine through, though often in a managed way. The last thing he wants to see is a "model home" and he's made his philosophy work for him as a successful realtor. So are all stagers coming to this conclusion?

Carla shook her head.

"With my clients, I *always* use the analogy of a model home. I actually *want* my staged homes to look and feel like model homes—a home that looks like nobody lives there. I want buyers to go in and envisage themselves living there, not spend their time trying to figure out who lives there now. That's why we do so much depersonalizing. In fact, many real model homes—the kind builders often present— are very 'decorated,' very full of stuff. But my sense is that stuff forces people to focus on stuff, not on the house and its architecture. It's a fine line, because I want homes to look inviting, but I want the potential buyer to experience the home for themselves, not through the seller. And if I can determine our likely buyer, I want to emphasize the features that would appeal to that buyer. If I think buyers will be attracted to hardwood floors, I want those floors to be seen.

But if it's a million-dollar property and an otherwise terrific kitchen has laminate countertops, I want to discuss changing them to granite. Why? Because buyers of expensive homes want granite."

I wondered how Carla dealt with the fact that the property might be viewed by a wide variety of potential buyers.

"First off, of course, we go neutral for that very reason. We try to keep it simple and classic, so the majority of buyers can appreciate the look. At the same time, we're sensitive to the character of the home. If it's a century-old Victorian house and we have to bring in furniture as part of the staging, we don't bring in highly contemporary-looking furniture. But we don't bring in outstanding vintage pieces either. We look at who's moving into and out of the neighbourhood and let that guide us. First-time buyers will likely have a preferred style. They may well want to raise kids there, so of course we'll emphasize the potential play area in the back yard. If the kitchen and the family area are connected, we'll highlight that fact because the parents will want to keep an eye on the children while preparing dinner. If we're in an upwardly mobile area, likely buyers are raising older children and want more space, more storage. In areas where retired folks tend to buy homes, these empty-nesters probably want less space but they can afford the amenities of a big house and they want those amenities."

"But you can't change the architecture of a house."

This was the basement of an older home," Carla remembered. "We decided to finish it because the house was on the smaller side and it would add more livable space, and also because buyers today want a home that is 'move-in ready'. Clearly finishing this basement would add value to the property. The challenge would be to show buyers that furniture could fit into this little, cold, uninviting space with its narrow stairway."

Carla understood from the start that unfinished basements can make houses hard to sell because of the 'move-in ready' factor. Buyers look at these basements and just picture work and trouble.

You can hardly tell this is the same room. The furniture demonstrates the room's potential and defines the space. The reds and greens transform it into a warm and cozy retreat

Carla said this home went on the market and sold within one week for 98% of list price.

"No, but we look carefully at things like floors, paint colours, furniture placement, lighting, We try to take everything into account and that's the basis of our discussions with the seller. Where should they invest?"

"You don't see it as a disadvantage that your houses looked staged, do you?"

"No no. The majority of buyers *want* the house to look staged. It tells them that small deficiencies have been corrected. It tells them the property has been through a *process*. If they see that the home hasn't been staged, they start to wonder what problems are hidden."

"So you see staging as a signal to the buyers that the house has been thoroughly prepared for the next owner?"

"That's right. Stagers aren't involved in the unethical business of hiding real problems. Alright, if the view isn't great, we probably won't emphasize it. We may put sheers across the window, but this doesn't deceive anyone. The buyers are free to look out the window. We stagers simply realize our job is to emphasize the positive and de-emphasize the negative." Darn it. That all sounded perfectly reasonable to me, so I asked Carla to walk me through a typical staging assignment.

"Well, as you know, we all start with a consultation and the consultation usually leads to the ultimate wish list. This is the list of things to do that if you did them all, the house would sell to the first viewer. But we rarely have the luxury of doing everything. There are always considerations of time and budget. Obviously, the longer lead time before the house goes on the market, the more opportunities to make helpful changes.

"For example, we recently had a house listed at 460,000 dollars—a fairly average price for a larger house in the Guelph area. It was built in the early 90s but hadn't been remodeled since. The look was tired but the agent didn't want too much done. He didn't want the dated kitchen cabinets painted, for instance. Anyway, I convinced the sellers and we spent the two weeks available repainting the whole interior—including those cabinets. The actual staging was very simple; the owner had a lot to work with. We brought in a few lamps and accessories, some bedding, I think. We went on the market and the house sold in four days for twenty-thousand dollars over list. The changes represented a great return on the owner's investment."

"I notice the agent didn't want too many changes."

"Well, remember, agents don't want to express negative opinions to their clients. That's *our* job. We're not the bad cop but we're the third voice the agent can depend on and smart agents know that. The agent's job is to build the relationship with the seller and to do what they do best: price the house, market it and see the sale through.

"The staging profession's relationship with real estate agents is a natural and it baffles me that some stagers spend time pursuing home owners. You as a home owner want to engage a realtor who works closely with a stager. It's this combination that makes sense.

"And as you know, Stephanie, even though mine is a one-person business, I often work with other stagers. When I have a bigger job and time is short, it's great to bring in colleagues who can work on one part of a house while I'm working on another. I know they'll do a great job and we'll finish in time. And they call on me when *they* need help. So these relationships are also a win-win for the seller.

"I do perhaps ten actual staging jobs a month not counting paid consultations. But these consultations are a critical part of the service. I go in, survey the house, and give my clients a clear description of what needs to be done. They may hire me to execute this plan in detail but they may also choose to follow my advice and do it themselves. Either way, it's great value for sellers at one hundred and twenty-five to four hundred dollars for a one-time consultation.

"You might find it strange that most realtors still don't avail themselves of this service, given the huge advantages. We talked about five percent of realtors using staging. But I have to agree with Kristy that the majority of realtors who don't use staging are largely that majority of realtors who don't sell a lot. If you as a stager are playing with the big boys, that two hundred dollar consultation fee is nothing to them. That why the five percent figure might be misleading.

It's not necessarily as little as five percent of transactions. The little guys don't do many transactions and they naturally want to keep as much of their commission as they can rather than invest it in their business by engaging a stager. But you, as a seller, must consider whether that's in *your* interest."

We wrapped up.

"Last question," I said. "Some people reading this book may be exposed to this staging thing for the first time. How would you describe the overall advantages of staging—in a nutshell?"

"The benefits?" she shook her head. "Astronomical. When you stage a home, you're targeting an audience and increasing the number of potential buyers. Your house shows better after staging and this may allow you and your agent to increase both your list and sale price. A realtor may say to the seller, 'If you do everything Carla recommends, I can list your house at 350,000 dollars. If you don't I won't be able to list it for more than 310,000 dollars.' That's a forty-thousand-dollar testimony to the power of staging. And if you sell within, say, thirty days rather than six months, how many mortgage payments have you saved?"

"And we have to remember how extremely stressful selling a house is," I said.

"Maybe only deaths and weddings are more stressful. The more you can prepare that house before it goes on the market, the quicker it's going to sell and the lower your stress. You can move on with your life, not waste it waiting."

I said good-bye to Carla. At this point, I was wondering if I needed to talk to any more of my colleagues. Hadn't I by now rung just about every variation of the theme?

No, as it turned out.

Jillian Summers: The Fully-Equipped Stager

Jillian Summers is a vital member of our Master-Mind group and a home stager living and working in London, Ontario, not that far from Guelph. London is an Ontario city of 366,000 people, home of Western University and often cited for a conservatism anchored in quite a lot of old wealth.

Jillian and I share a secret bond: we're both pretty shy. But she's become successful in a relatively short space of time, in part because of her obvious creativity. Her parents moved many times during her youth and looking at houses was the family hobby. Weekends would be spent touring model homes and commenting on décor. It was probably inevitable, as she told me, that she would feel comfortable in the housing field. As staging grew as a profession, her desire to join it grew stronger and stronger.

"I had a great job at a major insurance firm and of course I was reluctant to take the risk of leaving it. But I knew sitting in a cubicle was not really who I was and I finally summoned up my courage and resigned. It was sink or swim."

You don't have to know Jillian that well to realize she's not the business-averse, part-timer type that Kristy Morrison had encountered so often. With the assistance of her life partner, Nigel, and several friends interested in staging who act as project-specific contractors, she was going it alone. At the end of two years, she maintains a warehouse with, for example, eighty lamps and enough furniture to stage twelve vacant homes—maybe 100,000 dollars worth of inventory. there are probably only a couple of stagers in the London area using the warehouse-and-rent-out business model, which means she always has access to the staging props and accessories she needs.

"Karen said it wasn't really necessary to carry an inventory," I reminded her. She nodded in agreement.

"That's probably true in many cases. But if I want to do a house in a particular style and other stagers in town

What, you can imagine a buyer wondering, what would be the purpose of this little room? Passing through the house, it looks like any other. You can guess about its function, of course, but does that make you want it? The only selling point is the large window, which lets in a lot of natural light—appealing to many buyers. But without furniture the effect is cold and cramped. Jillian knew this was a critical issue.

Right away, anyone can see the room's purpose and potential for warmth and comfort: a guest room or a second bedroom. I'd make sure both lamps were turned on because even this tiny detail would brighten the room and showcase the picture. You could go further with the staging by pulling colours from the painting: blue, green or yellow accessories would give the space detail, "ground" the room and showcase the bedding.

Jillian told me that this home in London had been on the market for a year but the owners and their agent just couldn't find a buyer. The interior colours were good and there was a great fireplace, but the kitchen and large living room were all one and most buyers probably couldn't see past the empty space. As Jillian said, "It was imperative that we staged this so these rooms flowed properly."

I really like the way Jillian set up the furniture, symmetrical but not monotonously so, and tied in to the windows. The accessories brighten the picture and create eye appeal and the white couches are perfect, which wouldn't have been the case if the fireplace had been darker. Her accessories are seasonal and cheerful.

have rented all the available furniture in that style, I'm in a pickle."

"It's been a serious investment, though."

"It is, but upstaging seems to be thriving."

"I guess you're not one of the profession's many drop-outs."

"I can't afford that luxury," Jillian laughed. "I've put too much work into it. I think what happens is that people gain an impression from HGTV and other programs that staging is glamourous. When they enter the real world of staging work, when they find themselves in someone's house and see how hard the work is, it's a rude awakening. Staging isn't as dramatic and confrontational as TV portrays it, it isn't as quick and it isn't as simple. Stagers find themselves dealing with complex personal issues: the kids are running around maybe and the parent isn't well. People's homes are highly sensitive issues and you as a stager must be very careful. In fact this is something that has worried many real estate agents: they have nothing to gain from employing a rude or insensitive stager."

"Karen talked about being sensitive to buyer and seller."

"She's right."

"But what about stripping the house bare?" I asked. It seemed almost everyone had an opinion on this issue. "What about starting over versus allowing the owner's personality to show through?"

"I just had a consultation with a client this afternoon and we discussed that same issue," Jillian said. "I was explaining how we try to shape the home's image towards the most likely buyers. I was explaining how sometimes we just can't use a particular item that's in the house. I try to accommodate the owner's possessions but if I can't, the easiest thing is just to bring in a suitable piece from my warehouse.

"To be honest, I almost always have to bring in lamps and end tables and area rugs. I supply them because they're just not there."

"What sort of houses are we talking about?" I wondered.

"London's an older city by Canadian standards. For my business, we're usually talking about fifty-year-old suburban homes in the 175,000 dollar to 400,000 dollar range."

I was amazed. "You mean home owners in London, Ontario sometimes don't put bedside lamps in their spare bedrooms?"

"Far more often than not, they don't even put bedside lamps in their master bedrooms. People may want these accessories but they don't seem to get around to it."

As I was learning from my own experience too, the stager's work is never done.

"But even if I have to bring in lamps, carpets and sofas," she added, "in the majority of my assignments, the owners continue to live in the house. And they're generally pretty accepting of the changes. The only exception was the time I wanted the cats out so they wouldn't scratch my inventory. That was a problem."

We moved on to discussing the stager's constant challenge: to determine who will be the likely buyer. Without making that determination, stagers can't practice their art.

"First, I talk to the agent and get his ideas," Jillian said. "Then I look at the house. How big is it? How many bedrooms does it have? What neighbourhood is it in? Is it a ranch? A bungalow? A two-storey? Is it a condo? In a retirement area? I did a consultation today and will be doing a staging. It's an attached condo in a mixed neighbourhood but this particular complex is almost all retired couples. Retired couples have certain preferences. We'll be creating an office space in the spare upstairs bedroom. The basement is finished so we'll create a bedroom down there for visiting kids or grandkids. For the rest of the house I'll stay away from aggressively 'modern' styled furniture. I'll pick some accent colours and try to make them flow through the house."

We discussed the profession and its potential. Certainly not all stagers appreciate that potential. Remember the jealous competitiveness that Kristy described as a new stager?

"Yes, it's like going back to high school," Jillian confirmed. "But why should it be so cut-throat? The real potential is huge. There are probably fifteen hundred realtors in London. The staging profession is terribly under utilized. When I started, the first year, we staged nine homes. The second year, we did one hundred. Okay, this development has taken a great deal of discussion with agents to persuade them that the small additional cost of staging could produce a huge return, and yes, perhaps I've been lucky in that I'm working with some of the top-producing agents in this city, but when you consider the potential, it's almost humourous that stagers should view one another as competitors."

6.

Dream or Reality?

"Right," said Kristy. "But let's see if the shoe fits."

So in time—and in a sense—I came back to where I'd started. There was no one answer to the question of whether home staging consisted essentially of stripping a house of the seller's personality or leaving it for buyers to see and, hopefully, appreciate. Even Karen Schaeffer's wise observation that the goal of the stager is to sell the house as soon as possible at the best price (for the seller), true as it certainly is, somewhat begs the question: How do we do that?

There's no one answer because there's no one house, no one seller and no one buyer. Rules and guidelines and principles are helpful in understanding the staging process, but they're no substitute for the stager's art—part experience and part intuition. What are the rules for creating a significant piece of art—a poem, a painting, a musical composition? There are no such rules today and it's doubtful if there ever were.

That's not to say that I suggest you—I'm assuming you're a seller—should ignore all the advice you read here, there and elsewhere, or that you should think of us stagers as Patties, Stagers from Hell. Whatever philosophy informs their work, most stagers genuinely improve a home's salability, and the humblest and least experienced stager has the advantage enjoyed by the humblest and least experienced psycho-therapists: they're not *you* and they're not bound by your perspective.

I know before we start that not everything will apply to your home—in fact, most of it may not. But if you find in the course of our tour a half-dozen points and ideas that may not have occurred to you otherwise, it will be worth our time.

And before we set off, please, remember this most important fact: even if you paint your front door and dismantle your forty-three framed pictures of your children and wash every window inside and out, you're only half-way to really effective staging in what is becoming an increasing staged real estate market. The other half is that part of staging that's so hard to quantify: the delicate touches, the subtle effects, the nuanced nudges that go to create an emotional hook in your buyer.

That's where we stagers have a role to play. It's our forté.

A Final Consultation

I was sitting in my office. My desk was tidy and the laptop screen was glowing softly with an image of a house for sale. I had a few good prints on the wall and some tasteful furniture carefully placed around the room. Since my office had no ceiling, I looked up at the fluffy summer clouds that were floating by, then looked back down at the magazine I was reading and flipped the pages one by one. It was Architectural Digest but appeared to have been illustrated by a cartoonist, maybe the guy who draws The Simpsons. Anyway, the doorbell rang and a little woman came in and sat down in the chair opposite me. She didn't say a word but after a minute I noticed she was dabbing at her eyes with a hanky.

"Can I help you?" I asked finally.

She nodded. "Are you Stephanie?" she asked.

"Yes, I am."

"And you help people sell their homes?"

She sounded pretty distressed.

"That's right. I'm a home stager," I responded gently. "That's what we do."

> "Oh sure," I thought. "Like new owners these days want to start doing maintenance the moment they move in."

"Even houses that belong to old women?"

"You don't look that old to me, but yes—anyone."

"I can't sell my house!" she suddenly wailed. "Not to anyone!"

There was nothing to do but make us each a cup of tea and offer an oatmeal cookie for comfort. My visitor grew calmer and was able to introduce herself as Sarah Hubbard, a widowed single mom. When I asked her who had seen her house so far, she sighed deeply and put down her cup.

"My first potential was a young CEO. Very nice. He heads

up one of those software startups. His wife is in publishing. I thought they'd love my house but they looked uncomfortable. I offered them some freshly-baked pie but they left after five minutes."

"Really. Five minutes?"

"And then there was that man who owns two burger franchises in town. He and his wife, they got four children so I was sure they'd love my house."

"Did they?"

"Guess not. I saw them snickering in the hall. And then there was that there lovely dentist, Dr. Zylonsky. He made an appointment but he never even came in. I saw him sitting at the curb in his Porsche and he still sent me a bill for his time."

She began to weep again.

"Well, Mrs. Hubbard," I consoled her. "There there. Let's just take a look at your house. I'm sure we can do something."

"I hope so," Mrs. Hubbard sniffed.

"Shall we go right over then?"

She nodded. I took her hand and we rose straight up and out. This didn't seem surprising but it should have been a big clue that this was another dream. Still, you know how dreams are.

We floated over town, over some of the better suburbs where I assumed she lived. But no, we went on, until there were just woods and lakes below.

"This is pretty far out of the way," I thought.

"Just over there!" Mrs. Hubbard called.

I peered down and yes, by a little winding river that emptied into a darling little lake was a low little house with a high tower attached to one end.

"Um, Mrs. Hubbard," I said. I floated nearer to my new client and the two of us sort of came to a floating stop. Perhaps she sensed my hesitation because she looked at me in alarm.

"Mrs. Hubbard," I said. "You ... you appear to live in ... in a shoe."

"Now don't you start too!" she cried, almost turning upside down and beginning to dab again at her eyes.

"No no!" I said. "I mean, it's a really charming shoe-type home, but I think I'm going to have to call in my team. I don't think this is something I can do alone."

She looked up with apprehension. "Team?"

That's when the clouds parted and I saw the girls coming towards us straight out of the sun, riding the sunbeams. Karen was in front, blonde hair streaming, then Kristy laughing her head off, then Carla looking determined and Jillian bringing up the rear, lingering to admire the view.

They gathered around me, bobbing in the morning air. A tiny cloud drifted by and Karen waved away the vapours.

"You called?" she asked.

"Thank you," I said. "Mrs. Hubbard here lives down there in that shoe and she's had it on the market for ages."

I recounted the sad tale of buyers. "I think it's already obvious what the problem might be," I said.

"Right," said Kristy. "But let's see if the shoe fits."

So we swooped down and landed in the lovely garden—roses, delphinium, loads of hollyhock—with a dear little well and neatly trimmed lawns sloping down to the river. And all around us—kids. Kids were sliding down the creases in the toe and kids were climbing the chimney and kids were playing tag on the lawn.

"Whoa!" Carla said. "Mrs. Hubbard, are these ...?"

"Yes, yes." Mrs. Hubbard started sniveling again. "Yes, I got so many children I don't know what to do."

Karen looked around. "Well, first, count your lucky stars you didn't contact Patty, the Stager from Hell. You contacted Stephanie instead. Stephanie?"

"Mrs. Hubbard," I said softly. "Do you realize that this is a school day?"

"School" She looked puzzled.

"Nowadays we have fine public education systems. All your children should be in school, learning about gender politics and other subjects."

Her eyes widened. "Not running all over the house and laughing?"

"Not really. And you know what? Children sometimes

spook buyers. They're a blessing in every home but just more personality than a home for sale needs."

With that, we entered through a wooden door just in front of the heel and I don't think I saw a child again.

"Charming!" Jillian cried. She was looking at the beautiful "folk" paintings that decorated every inch of woodwork. "Normally I'd discourage very, er, individual art like this, but here it works."

"They're what my dear departed husband did for me," Mrs. Hubbard said. "That and fourteen children. See, that's artists for you every time. They're great 'cept for the money."

"I hear you," said Jillian.

"Awesome!" I heard Kristy muttering. She'd gone forward towards the toe and I could see her admiring the many carefully wrought and curtained bunk beds, no doubt also the work of Mr. Hubbard. She peered out through the leaded window that filled the space where the toe was peeled back. "This place has sole!" she cackled.

"Now, Mrs. Hubbard." Karen looked serious. "Stephanie and I have been talking and we're all agreed. This is a clear case of not understanding your buyer."

"I got none—none!" Mrs. Hubbard wailed.

"But every house has a buyer," I soothed.

"We just have to figure out who they are," Jillian added.

So we all sat down at the cozy table, which was not a toadstool exactly but something nice and gnarly that Mr.

Hubbard had fashioned, and I explained how Mrs. Hubbard had been pitching her house as a primary residence for fairly well-heeled (no pun) buyers. But in fact, such buyers would never live in a distant shoe, no matter how great the view. What she had, I explained, was a perfect recreational home—a cottage—for people who loved the outdoors and a load of rustic charm. And here was the really good news I had for her: My whole ambition was to become a stager of recreational homes!

"Put us to work, Stephanie!" Karen called. She was already rolling up her sleeves and the others were doing the same. In a twinkling we'd all set to work, rushing from room to room, tidying away clutter, packing up thirteen hundred and forty-one photos of children, oiling leather siding and brass hinges, washing the round lace hole windows, nailing down loose floor boards, sweeping the patio platform on the roof that afforded a terrific view of the river. Carla threw open the doors to the big cupboards that lined both walls. They were empty.

"Wait a minute," she said, turning to Mrs. Hubbard. "Wait a minute. You ever have a dog, ma'm?"

"Oh yes." Mrs. Hubbard was dabbing at her eyes again. "He was a wonderful dog. Wonderful. Knew all sorts of tricks. I'd go out to buy him some fruit, and when I'd come back, he'd be playing the flute. I'd go out to buy him some tripe and..."

"And he died, right?"

"Yes, he died," she sniffed. "Couldn't afford to keep him alive."

"Because the cupboards were all bare, right?" asked Carla.

"That's true."

"Mother Hubbard," Karen came forward. "Do you realize what this means?"

My client shook her head.

"It means," Karen said. "It means"—and here we all joined her in unison—"It means plenty of room for storage!" And we cheered together.

"Now all we need is someone who knows that sort of buyer," I said.

"And behold! He is among you!" came a voice from outside. I looked up and there was Craig, of all people, his nose pressed against the glass window that was once a giant's lace hole. A moment later, he was in the room.

"When Pilgrim is here, buyers are near!" he cried.

"Craig!" I said. "Gosh!"

"Awesome!" Kristy said. She comes from Ontario, where really dashing realtors are harder to find.

"You really have a buyer for this place?" Carla asked, looking a little suspicious.

Craig flipped through his iPhone.

"Hmm. Shoe. Shoe. Yes, here he is. 'Will consider shoe. Or stalk.' Not sure what that means but I'm onto him now."

He began to punch a number into his phone when the door burst open.

"Don't bother!" cried an attractive woman in a voice tinged with Spanish. "Don't bother! I've got him first!"

I realized with a shock it was Chona dela Cruz, holding a small sturdily-built, balding man by the ear.

"Chona!" I stammered. "I...I thought you didn't use stagers!"

"I love stagers!" Chona said, dropping the small man on a chair. "I love them when they're free. Anyway, this gentleman loves this house. His name is Jack."

Craig peered at his iPhone. "That's right," he said. "His name is Jack." He turned to me with a rueful smile. "Well," he said. "It's a competitive business. You can't win 'em all."

Jack looked around the room with a huge grin.

"By golly, Chona, thank you!" he chortled. "I'll be forever grateful, eh? I've always admired this house from above, even without a curb, eh? Even admired it when it was on the foot of the giant, may he rest. Now I'll admire it from the inside 'cause it has everything I want. It's warm, bright, clean, uncluttered, full of personality."

"See?" Craig said. "That's staging for you."

"He can afford it too," said Chona. "Since his mother died."

"My dear old mom has passed, eh?" Jack shook his head. "Course, she always loved the castle but what's the use of holding on to that place now?"

"Really? You have a castle?" Karen raised an eyebrow. "I'm quite interested in high-end homes. Where is it?"

"Actually,"—Jack's eyes were sparkling—"Actually, it's in the Air, eh?"

"I've heard of that," Carla said. "I don't think it's such a great neighbourhood."

"Anyway, I've got bags of money, so no problem," said Jack. "Bags. I just want ..." Then he stopped, his mouth open. "Who is this beautiful woman?" he asked and his voice dropped to hardly more than a whisper.

"I'm the owner," said Mrs. Hubbard. "The former owner. Sellin' only by necessity."

Jack glided around the table to the chair beside her.

"My dear," he said, taking her hand. "Could I presume you to be the widow Hubbard?"

"I am," said Mrs. Hubbard. "Fourteen kids but all in school. And no dog."

"I allergic to dogs and I'm buying your house this instant," said Jack. "And never mind the price. But would you ever consider me?"

"Consider you?"

"As a husband, I mean?"

Mrs. Hubbard gave him a sharp look. "If you're presentable, yes, I suppose I might, if you happen to ask me. But there'd be no giant killing. And no stalk climbing and no

slipping beans to the kids, either."

"Awesome," said Kristy.

That's when I noticed the light fixture. It seemed to be getting clearer. I blinked once or twice and realized it was the fixture on my bedroom ceiling. Light was streaming in through the curtains. I sighed.

Another flawless staging assignment successfully completed.

The Appendices

We stagers can only help those who help themselves.

Appendix 1
Your Personal Walk-Through

I'd like to leave you with a final tour of a house for sale—your house perhaps—and a quick checklist of the best advice I and other stagers offer. These are the things you can often do yourself, whether or not you engage the services of a professional stager who will give your home that something special that will set it above all the others. I'm indebted for this checklist to HGTV's *Front Door* and have added my own suggestions where I've thought they'd help.

1. Plan Ahead

   • Walk through each room and criticize the home from a buyer's perspective.

   • Ask a few local real estate professionals for their advice.

   • Consider getting a professional home inspection to see if any repairs are needed.

   • Hire a contractor to handle any major projects.

   • Consider getting an appraisal to find out your current market value.

   • Hold a yard sale. Sell, donate or trash anything you don't need.

2. Clean, Declutter and Depersonalize

I know you've heard enough about this, but just by way of review:

- Thoroughly clean your entire home.

- Scrub tile in the kitchen and bathrooms.

- Clean hardwood floors.

- Steam clean carpets and drapes. Consider replacing carpet if stains are prominent.

- Get rid of all dust bunnies.

- Repair cracks and holes in the walls.

- Paint interior walls with neutral colors, like beige, cream or light pastels. Pale blues and greens are good for bathrooms.

- Remove excess and oversized furniture.

- Rearrange furniture to maximize space.

- Organize room closets and store out-of-season clothes.

- Remove all small appliances, toys, magazines and pet items.

- Remove most family photos, personal collections and medications.

- Remove items from the garage and store them off site.

- Secure valuable items, including cash and jewelry.

3. Your Home from the Curb

- Power wash your siding and windows. Only then will you really know if you must proceed to the next step.

- Check and if necessary repaint your house's exterior, including trim, doors and shutters. Cost is a factor if we're talking about the actual siding, but never underestimate the magic of a coat of paint.

- Step back and look at that front door, doorbell, address number and welcome mat. Are they absolutely flawless, as the gateway to your home?

- Repair any cracks in the driveway and sidewalks.

- Sweep the entryway and walkways.

- Mow, water and fertilize the lawn.

- Store any toys or equipment lying on the yard.

- Clean up pet droppings.

- Clean the gutters and downspouts.

- Trim shrubs and trees and rake the leaves.

- Plant flowers and shrubs.

Your plantings should be those that can survive the weather in your area and that will complement the structure and colouring of the house and bring focus to the best features. In some drastic cases, you might want to call a landscape architect into action. A really first-class landscape architect may consider botany, horticulture, visual art, industrial design, geography, ecology and environmental psychology in developing a landscape plan for your property. This is generally overkill for most homes for sale, but as always, expenditures must be judged by their ultimate effect on the property's selling price.

4. The Kitchen Tour

Let's face it: your kitchen can make or break your sale. If your prospective buyer happens to be a serious home cook or entertainer. the kitchen will be doubly important to them.

To start, there are a few basic tasks that no seller, however modest, can afford to ignore.

- Mop and wax/polish your floors.

- Clear the countertops.

- Replace outdated hardware.

- Clean appliances and fixtures.

- Clean and organize the pantry, cabinets and drawers.

Needless to say, you can go far beyond this and just as people sometimes go too far in spending on their kitchens, a home seller can exceed the mandate too. We must always remember: the first principle of home staging is to sell the home at the best price in the shortest time. When we do forty-thousand dollar kitchen remodelings to add twenty thousand dollars to our selling price, we haven't done well. Nonetheless, sometimes it makes sense to do more than the minimum. If we're thinking about bigger changes, it may do no harm to call in a kitchen remodeling professional who can suggest how best to use presently wasted space to eliminate that waste and improve the flow of movement.

You can get away with dim, atmospheric lighting

elsewhere in the house, but the kitchen demands strong overhead lighting that eliminates shadows. That lighting will reveal imperfections, though, so get ready to make some improvements.

Countertops and their brethren, the cabinets, are first to fall under the spotlight and of course they're important to everyone, both in respect to the choice of materials and their uncluttered presentation. Somehow, the wear and tear of years on these surfaces, well lit, can really turn off home buyers. You might simply choose to thoroughly clean and refinish your existing cabinets, remove the doors to create an impression of openness, install new high-quality hardware, or even replace the cabinets altogether. As always, it's a cost/benefit calculation. But make no mistake: the modern kitchen is the hub of the modern home.

By the way, don't forget the lowly backsplash, the area between the countertop and the bottom of the cabinets or window sill. Grease accumulates here, with splatters of sauce, dust and grime. Scour it ruthlessly but if that's to no avail, resist the temptation to paint it. Backspashes seldom take paint well and it's probably better to replace a battered one with one made of a resistant material that will not date too quickly.

You probably won't sell your refrigerator with your house but many homes are sold with stoves and sinks built in.

5. Your Bathroom

Like the kitchen, huge attention is often devoted to the fitting out and decoration of bathrooms. Likewise, home buyers will pay bathrooms special attention.

- Examine and replace stained or defective caulking around the sinks and bathtubs.

- Remove stains from sinks, toilets and bathtubs.

- Keep all toilet seat lids closed.

- Hang fresh towels.

To be fair, the bathroom is probably the most used room in any home and the familiar staging rules of attractiveness, easily discernible flow and adequate storage space apply. In extreme cases, where sellers feel that remodeling is necessary and financially justified, I'd recommend a professional bathroom specialist to bring the design of the bathroom up to modern standards. A good designer can create a luxurious spa atmosphere in the master bath that will bypass any buyer's rational faculties and might even sell the house all on its own.

6. Up on the Roof

What's a loose shingle going to cost to repair? What's it going to cost in the final selling price of your house?

You might as well be prepared: Most homebuyers are going to ask about the roof when looking at a home. The roof is a home's critical defense against the elements and, alas, about the most costly element requiring inevitable replacement. If your roof is old or damaged, it's best to face reality and address the problem before putting your home on the market.

As a first step, you might want to call (several, not one) licensed roofing contractors. these specialists will evaluate your roof and give you an estimate of the repair or replacement work that needs to be done.

A roofing contractor normally begins by looking at the ceilings for signs of water damage, then enters the attic to do a thorough inspection of the roof decking (the material layer that ties all the structural components together). The decking should show no evidence of sagging, dark spots, trails, or signs of leaking. Oh yes: there should be no light showing through either.

The contractor then goes go up on the roof and inspects for signs of aging:

- damage to shingles or shakes, bare spots, cracking, blistering, warping, curling or splitting of tiles

- looseness of the granular coating of shingles and or shingle granules in the gutters

- algae growth or other signs of rot or mold

- wear and tear around roof features (chimneys, vents, pipes, etc.)

- flashing damage (flashing a thin piece of sheet metal used to prevent water from leaking in at angles or joints in the roofing.

- gutters and downspouts that are loose and dangling or full of debris such that they don't allow proper drainage

- damage from termites

Of course, it's much less expensive to repair a roof than to replace it, and if the damage is minimal, due to weathering rather that failure of materials, and if the sub-surface structure does not show significant moisture, a repair may be all you require to deflect a buyer's concerns. A general rule of thumb is: thirty percent damage or more and the roof must be replaced. Depending on the type of damage, it may be less expensive to replace than keep repairing.

If you decide to install a new roof, hiring a professional is the best option for most owners. Roofs are dangerous environments to start with and there are important limits on materials depending on the house's structure, your climate and other local conditions. A little tip, though: New materials can sometimes be placed over the old roofing materials. This can save the cost of tearing off the old roof and add protection. But never more than two layers on the roof!

7. Appealing to the Senses

- Bake cookies or burn scented candles.

- Offer light refreshments.

- Install higher wattage incandescent light bulbs to brighten rooms but generally avoid overhead lighting, which washes out colours. Lamps are the most reliable and flattering lighting in most rooms except kitchen and bathroom.

- Turn on all the lights.

- Open windows to let in fresh air.

- Open curtains or blinds to let in natural light and show off views.

- Turn off TVs.

- Relocate pets on the day of the open house.

- Refrain from smoking in your home.

8. Showing Off Your Home's Best Features

- If you have hardwood floors, remove rugs to show those floors off.

- You probably won't be selling your drapes. Pull them back to showcase nice views (if you have nice views).

- Stage the front porch or deck with furniture and potted plants.

- Make sure fireplaces are in working condition.

- Clean the backyard and pool area.

9. Prepare for Your Open House

- Hold an exclusive brokers' open house to let local agents know your home is on the market. Offer food and refreshments.

- Inform family, friends and neighbors of the date and time of your open house.

- Put ads in local newspapers, real estate publications and on free web sites such as Craigslist.com.

- Put up "Open House" signs on the front lawn and at nearby intersections with directions to the house.

- Create property description sheets and prepare important documents, such as homeowner's association rules, inspection reports and purchase offer forms.

If you're a seller, remember that the more special instructions are attached to showing a home, the more reluctant an agent may be to include it in his or her showings. If there are several homes of equal appeal on the market in an area where a buyer is interested, the agent will show those that have fewer showing restrictions first.

The ideal is to show your home any time without warning between 9:00 A.M. and 9:00 P.M. However, this is almost never a realistic option because sellers most often live in the home and have kids and pets. Your agent will try to accommodate almost any schedule but the more restrictions placed on showings, the less often a house is likely to be shown.

If you have pets, you'll want to have some warning before a showing so you can relocate Fluffy and Bowser temporarily. Adorable as they are, leaving them in the house during a showing is the least desirable of options.

Appendix 2
Home Staging as a Profession

Home staging is the process of evaluating a property and revamping it in order to get a higher selling price and a quicker sale. Having an outsider look at your property with impartial eyes and evaluate what needs to be done to achieve this objective can mean the difference between an early sale at a higher price and a house that sits on the market for months (or years).

Barb Schwarz coined the term "staging" in 1972 in Bellevue, Washington. As a real estate agent, Schwarz realized she needed to attract more potential buyers and keep them engaged in the process. Of course most sellers already realized they needed to paint and buy new bed covers when they put their houses on the market, but that was not enough for Schwarz, who developed and systemized her approach, then in 1985 began to market it as a training program for stagers. She is credited with having founded the staging profession.

Home Staging Training and Associations

Today there is a profusion of home staging training available. Here are some of the better known groups.

The International Association of Home Staging Professionals: IAHSP

Barb Schwarz went on to found the International Association of Home Staging Professionals in 1999. The founder stresses that the association is part of the real estate industry and not the interior decorating and home designing professions.

Schwarz's Accredited Staging Professional course is usually three days of intense training on staging. Participants must pass an extensive written test and agree to abide by the ASP Code of Ethics and the ASP Consumer Foundation of Service Creed. Graduates receive accreditation as an Accredited Staging Professional and are eligible to take the Accredited Staging Professional Masters Course. The Masters Course consists of five twelve-hour days of intensive work packed with exercises to teach the finer points of operating a home staging business.

The Association of Property Scene Designers: APSD

The Association of Property Scene Designers, APSD, was founded by Karen Schaefer as a certified staging, business and marketing solution for the home staging industry. Today, APSD has clients and followers in fourteen countries.

APSD offers Certified Home Staging training classes, both online and live along with the business and marketing classes that every home stager needs in order to run a successful home staging business.

Online certified trainings are self-paced, home study courses that can be completed in the stagers own time. They cover home staging, marketing, curb appeal, color analysis and many other home staging topics.

Live certified trainings are offered in a two-, three- or four-day format covering everything from time management, business structure, effective and easy marketing, promotion, building a team and hand's-on home-staging training.

All courses are supported with monthly complimentary trainings, live Q and A sessions, one-on-one support and a worldwide private networking site: www.APSDmembers.com

Home Staging Resources: HSR

Home Staging Resources is an online training program for certification in home staging and redesign. The company's mission is "to add credibility and integrity to the home staging and redesign industry" through their training programs which feature a twenty-one day comprehensive training program for home stagers.

Certified Staging Professionals
International Business Training Academy

The International Business Training Academy (CSP) was founded by Christine Rae in 2001. Ms. Rae has developed the curriculum and has promoted her field by participating on television reality shows featuring staging of homes for sale. Ms. Rae, is also president of the Canadian Staging Professionals Association.

The CSP training consists of a three-day course: two days of classroom instruction and one day of field instruction. This is followed by a four-week follow-up of home study. There are also six webinars available on marketing your staging business.

The CSP training is designed to appeal to home stagers the world over and has trained many in the international community especially in Canada and Australia.

The Real Estate Staging Association

The Real Estate Staging Association is an organization to advance the profession of home staging. The association does not offer training, but constitutes a resource agency for stagers, maintaining directories of training organizations, home stagers, resources for stagers, and other information vital to the operation of a staging business. The RESA also offers consumers a platform for lodging comments and complaints regarding their experience with member stagers.

Interior Redesign

An offshoot of the home staging industry is interior redesign. Unlike home staging, interior redesign uses the furniture, artwork and accessories already in the home to transform it into something more desirable and more likely to appeal to buyers. It gives the property a different look at little added cost.

The Spread of Staging

The trend to home staging began in California and spread eastwards in the United States and Canada. In the UK, Australia, the Czech Republic, Spain, Ireland, Austria, Poland, France and Italy, there is growing awareness of the benefits of home staging, with realtors and sellers increasingly embracing the practice. As elsewhere, the process begins with higher end property owners availing themselves of the service. As the value is realized, others joining the trend.

We're now seeing staging in Japan, China, Korea, Malaysia, and Vietnam using concepts from Asian cultures to improve the flow of a home and attract buyers. And of course, here in the West, designers and stagers are employing Asian themes in their staging to foster the calm and peaceful atmosphere associated with Asian design.

Locally, in Edmonton, interest in staging is also growing. Realtors who have never used staging are considering it on a daily basis. Why? The market is highly competive and without staging, houses are sitting on the market longer. Staged houses

- Sell quicker
- Get multiple offers
- Sell for higher prices than they would otherwise
- Staging is becoming a viable option.

Final Thoughts

If you have any questions, or if you need my assistance with any staging challenge, I'd be delighted to help you. Contact me at (780) 991-6723 or e-mail me at Stephanie Lycka <stephanie.lycka@gmail.com>. I'll do my best to respond to your requests.

About the Author

Stephanie Lycka was born and raised in Edmonton, Alberta and studied residential interiors at the University of Alberta and home staging with Karen Schaefer at the Association of Property Scene Designers (APSD). She is an APSD Certified Residential Interiors Specialist, a Certified Luxury Property Specialist, a Certified Stager Pro, a Certified Home Stager and a Certified Colour Specialist.

The People in this Book

Chona dela Cruz, realtor
RE/MAX Elite
Unit 17, 8103 – 127 Avenue
Edmonton, Alberta
T5C 1R9 Canada
780-406-4000
http://www.chonasells.com

Craig Pilgrim, realtor
ComingHome Real Estate
RE/MAX Real Estate
12 Hebert Road St. Albert,
AB T8N 5TB
780-458-8300
http://www.cominghome.ca

Carla Woolnough, property styler
Nex-Step Design
Guelph, Ontario
519-957-2703
http://www.nex-stepdesign.com

Kristy Morrison, home stager
Capital Home Staging and Design
5450 Canotek Road Unit #68
Ottawa, ON
K1J 9H4
613-832-8958
http://capitalhomestaginganddesign.ca

Karen Schaefer, home staging trainer
Association of Property Scene Designers
PO Box 271
Manitou Springs, CO 80829
1-877-900-7824
http://www.apsdmembers.com

Jillian Summers, home stager
UpStaging
London, Ontario
519-317–5533
http://www.upstaginghomes.com

Jack and Mrs. Hubbard
Found that the shoe fit and wore it happily
ever after as a direct result of a successful
staging.

CPSIA information can be obtained at www.ICGtesting.com
Printed in the USA
LVOW02s0738051013

355505LV00001B/1/P

9 781927 664032